UNDERSTANDING
LLOYD'S
A GUIDE TO CORPORATE MEMBERSHIP

The editor and understanding Lloyd's

Iain Simpson started working in the Lloyd's market over thirty years ago and has since gained wide experience in the London, U.S. and Bermuda insurance markets. He has spent the last ten years acting in an advisory capacity to Lloyd's Names and became a name himself in 1988.

The timely decision by Lloyd's to introduce corporate membership in 1994 – breaking a three hundred year tradition – was the catalyst for writing this book. Having spent many years explaining the complexities of Lloyd's to Names without the help of a central work of reference, it was evident that introducing a book which brought together all the strands of what is clearly a complex market, would be a welcome reference source not only for prospective corporate members but anyone else with an interest in Lloyd's.

Iain recently left the Sedgwick Members Agency where he was the Marketing Director and now runs a marketing consultancy, focusing on the insurance market and other professional services. He also provides a consultancy to existing and prospective names on membership issues, particularly incorporation.

UNDERSTANDING
LLOYD'S
A GUIDE TO CORPORATE MEMBERSHIP

Roden Richardson

Edited by Iain C. Simpson

Quiller Press
London

Contents

~CONTENTS~

~CONTENTS~

~CONTENTS~

Introduction

Lloyd's is one of the strongest brand names in the world. Those who have no direct connection with the market but know enough not to confuse it with the bank, understand it is "to do with insurance" but do not necessarily have any idea beyond that how the market derives its business, deals with it and organises its supply of capital. Once a general appreciation of these facts is known, the observer will be impressed by the global spread of business that is underwritten through an extraordinary network of intermediaries and, despite the recently well-publicised problems, the high-esteem in which the name "Lloyd's" is still held around the world.

"Understanding Lloyd's: A Guide to Corporate Membership" gives the reader a clear and in-depth understanding of how Lloyd's operates. The complexities of the market together with its procedures, rules and regulations are explained in detail making the Guide both an effective learning tool and a valuable reference book. It is the first comprehensive work dealing with the structure and operation of Lloyd's that has been published since Lloyd's opened its doors to Corporate Capital in 1994.

This Guide was inspired by the arrival of this new class of capital, which ended more than 300 years of tradition by allowing underwriting to be conducted on a limited liability basis. Historically, Lloyd's capital has been provided solely from the funds of private individuals, who, under English law as sole traders, are subject to unlimited liability.

With the continued support of many wealthy Names who still represent 55% of the market's capital, the significant participation by Corporate investors and, most important, the future market now separated from past liabilities, there is every reason to expect a healthy future for this historic market.

Iain C. Simpson

Acknowledgments

The "Understanding Lloyd's" project was originally intended for completion at a much earlier date. However, the programme to restructure the Lloyd's market has been so thorough and extensive that it is only now, after the most recent changes to corporate capital rules, that the time seems right finally to go to print.

No project like this would ever come to fruition without the enthusiastic help and assistance from a wide range of talented people. In particular I would like to give my thanks to Roden Richardson, who authored the main text and gave such good foundation to the guide, and to a considerable number of individuals in Lloyd's whose help and enthusiasm carried this project to, what I hope they think is, a satisfactory conclusion.

Recent Developments at Lloyd's

'Reconstruction and Renewal'

The book would not be complete without reference to the Reconstruction and Renewal programme (R&R), which was successfully completed in the latter part of 1996 after more than two years of hard work. Lloyd's embarked on the R&R programme after the market recorded significant insurance losses in the 1988 to 1992 years of account.

The Problem

The years 1989 and 1990 were particularly heavily hit with catastrophe losses. As a result of the way in which the reinsurance market had developed in previous years, an accumulation of these catastrophe losses ended up in a relatively small number of syndicates which became known as 'spiral syndicates'. During this period there was also significant over-capacity which led to a very weak rating structure in most markets and policies being written on imprudently wide terms and conditions. Perhaps of a more insidious and potentially damaging nature was the problem of the 'old years' liabilities which were the liabilities inherited from prior years of account and which were causing major concerns amongst the Membership because of the need to constantly increase premium reserves against those liabilities. An increasing lack of confidence grew from this and accelerated the collapse of many syndicates in the market, resulting in a reduction from over 400 to 170 within the space of four years. This left a huge accumulation of 745 open years of account, on which thousands of Members were trapped with no immediate prospect of a resolution of this immense problem.

The combination of all these factors began to cause acute financial pressure on the Lloyd's market and started to call into question the ability of the Central Fund to withstand the increasing pressures. Other major factors were: an increasing amount of litigation by Names against Managing and Members' Agents, mostly over alleged cases of negligent underwriting; increasing concern in the United States amongst insurance regulators as to the future viability of Lloyd's and an increasing damage to client confidence. This was possibly the first time in the history of Lloyd's that the security of Lloyd's policies had been called seriously into question.

The Solution

The R&R programme therefore became synonymous with resolving the problems of the past, the reconstruction of finances of the market and the rebuilding of Lloyd's. The cornerstone of the Lloyd's Reconstruction plan was the formation of Equitas, a reinsurance company specifically created to reinsure all the liabilities still outstanding on 1992 and prior years of account for all Lloyd's syndicates. If successful, this proposal would take away the majority of the problem open years of account and provide traditional Names with what was termed as 'affordable finality'. It was widely recognised that the success of Equitas would largely rely on the quality of reserving that would be put in place to ensure its viability and at the same time the need to satisfy the requirements of the UK Department of Trade and Industry (DTI). However, to satisfactorily resolve the problems of the past, the other vital element needed was a settlement of the litigation that had increasingly been mounted by Names against Lloyd's Members' and Managing Agents and which during the course of 1995 and early 1996 had proved to be increasingly successful. It was quite clear that the Action Groups of Names who were litigating, or proposing to do so would not be satisfied unless the Settlement Offer was substantially greater that the £900m of the first offer which they had summarily rejected in 1994.

The basic proposition offered in the R&R document issued in May 1995 was a total offer of £2.8 billion. This was made up of £2 billion in debt credits and £800 million as an out-of-court settlement to litigants. Added to this was the prospect of a normal pay-out from the 1993 account profit and also advanced payments from the 1994 and 1995 account, all of which were anticipated to be very profitable. Also included in the proposition was a strengthening of central finances and an additional levy on Names of approximately £450 million.

In March 1996, the DTI issued an authorisation of Equitas Reinsurance Ltd which was subject to certain conditions, the main one of which was that sufficient premium at a level satisfactory to the DTI should be available to Equitas Reinsurance Ltd. This to a large degree depended on the number of names accepting the Lloyd's settlement offer and assets collected from other sources including Lloyd's underwriting agencies and brokers.

The original forecast additional premium requirement from names for Equitas of £1.9 Billion was subsequently reduced to £859 Million. This allowed Lloyd's to increase the total value of the settlement offer to around £3.2 Billion and also provide more assistance to those names who had paid all their Lloyd's obligations and at the same time those who faced the greatest financial difficulty.

Lloyd's settlement offer succeeded and the DTI's authorisation of Equitas Reinsurance Ltd became unconditional on 3.9.96.

The success of the Reconstruction Plan thus hinged on achieving wide-spread settlement of litigation. The complexity of this undertaking should not be underestimated. The negotiating team at Lloyd's had to deal with the often conflicting interests of more than 50 litigating groups of Lloyd's Members and their legal representatives, market Underwriters, Lloyd's agents, brokers and their auditors. It is a huge credit to all involved that in spite of the disparity of views and the conflicts that the discussions have borne fruit. Perhaps the most interesting factor is that the settlement had gradually been shaped by negotiation with the Membership rather than by an arbitrarily imposed central process.

A vital ingredient enabling Lloyd's to achieve acceptance of the Settlement Offer has been the unprecedented profits generated from the 1993/1994 and 1995 (forecast) years of accounts, the forecast collective profit of which amounts to approximately £3 billion. In addition, Lloyd's has retained the support of the vast majority of its client base and has demonstrated a resilience that by all comparisons would be considered remarkable.

CHAPTER ONE

A brief history of Lloyd's

Lloyd has always been a familiar surname in Britain. It is scarcely surprising, then, that in the 17th century a certain London coffee house should have been owned and managed by a Mr Lloyd. Somewhat more surprising, though, is that this same man would pass on the use of his name to an organisation which was born at least in part as a result of the way he served coffee – and which would eventually become a world-famous byword for reliable insurance.

Mr Lloyd's Coffee House was one of hundreds in the capital which had sprung up to cater for the popularity of the pungent new drink recently brought back to Europe from the New World. London was then already an important port and rapidly becoming a major trading centre. Unlike the noisy taverns, the city's coffee houses had become an ideal place in which to do business; Lloyd's was frequented by merchants and the shipping fraternity.

An important part of their dealings was to obtain insurance for their ships and cargoes, and a particular reason for choosing Mr Lloyd's coffee house was that he took as much trouble over the quality of the shipping news available in his establishment as he did over his coffee – a particular advantage in view of the importance of reliable news and information for successful underwriting. The significance of Mr Lloyd's reporting abilities is brought home when it is remembered that this was a time before the invention of formal news-gathering and newspapers. In fact *Lloyd's List* is the world's oldest daily international newspaper, first published in 1788.

Nearly a century later, the more discerning and reputable customers of Lloyd's Coffee House (as it was still called) broke away and set up "New Lloyd's Coffee House". Unlike the earlier establishment, where insurance was sometimes simply another word for betting, this was devoted strictly to marine insurance. However, it soon proved too small and, as business developed, special rooms were leased in the Royal Exchange nearby. By this time the informal association of merchants, underwriters and brokers had formed the Society which would evolve directly into today's organisation. In 1871, Lloyd's, as the Society was now universally known, was incorporated by an Act of Parliament; this provided the legal foundation which enabled it to make laws backed by the full authority of Parliament.

In the century preceding its incorporation, Lloyd's had been tested to the full by events such as the American War of Independence, a twenty-two year war with France and, starting in 1824, by competition from the newly emancipated insurance company market. It was not found wanting. Its business base expanded from the marine insurance upon which it was founded to become a market where almost any insurable risk could be covered.

In the century or more that followed, five further Acts of Parliament were required to keep pace with Lloyd's success and in 1982, after lengthy debate, the Council of Lloyd's was created.

Soon afterwards, with three centuries of successful trading behind it, Lloyd's, like the insurance industry in general, was suddenly overtaken by large losses. These resulted from an unprecedented chain of claims caused by a unique combination of natural disasters, environmental pollution and some unwise underwriting by a handful of syndicates. To maintain its reputation for reliability, a fundamental review of operations was undertaken in 1992, resulting in a new business plan the following year. This plan set out a radical programme to resolve the inherited problems of the past, particularly the "old years" problem and outstanding legal disputes. Implementation of the plan has introduced strong central direction to what is in effect a multiplicity of small or medium sized businesses. By adopting this direct management approach to building a new Lloyd's with higher professional standards, more independent regulation and lower costs, the first important steps have been taken to creating a new Lloyd's capable of addressing the needs of its international clients into the next century.

CHAPTER TWO

The Lloyd's Market

AN OUTLINE

Lloyd's of London is not a company but a market. It therefore has no shareholders and accepts no corporate liability. Dedicated to insuring risk, it has been active in the City of London for over 300 years (*see outline history*, previous chapter).

Protecting the policy-holder

Lloyd's has an internationally renowned ability to respond quickly, innovatively and effectively to complex, hazardous and often unusual risks. It maintains a leading position in the world's marine, aviation and reinsurance markets. In its chosen arenas of business it has traditionally set the standards for insurance policy pricing, terms and conditions. About half of all London international insurance market business is underwritten at Lloyd's; for almost two-thirds, its underwriters take the lead role. While these achievements reflect its expertise and experience, they are also closely connected with Lloyd's unique structure and mode of operation.

In brief, the Lloyd's market has, until the recent introduction of Corporate Membership, traditionally consisted of thousands of sole traders individually seeking profit – and, through the operation of English law, consequently shouldering unlimited liability for any losses. The traders participate in the market by joining syndicates whose underwriters accept risks in exchange for premiums through brokers representing policyholders – the ultimate customers.

As a market, Lloyd's is thus essentially what you would expect: a collection of independent entities competing for business. The market's efficiency and effectiveness for the conduct of insurance business is confirmed by three centuries of sustained growth and success – and an untarnished reputation for meeting the legitimate claims of the insurance policyholders it ultimately serves.

To appreciate how Lloyd's works and how its Members participate it helps to look at it in terms of two main parts: governance and operation.

GOVERNANCE

Society, Council and Boards

Governance of Lloyd's is achieved through the Council of Lloyd's and Lloyd's

Regulatory and Market Boards. The Council was set up as a result of the 1982 Act of Parliament and is responsible for the management and supervision of the Society of Lloyd's Members (itself created by Act of Parliament in 1871). The Council has the right to exercise the powers of the Society and regulates and directs the business of insurance at Lloyd's. It also has substantial disciplinary powers.

The Market Board develops and implements Lloyd's market strategy and the provision of central services; the Regulatory Board attends to the regulation of the market. Both Boards were created in 1993 to help strengthen management. More details about the Council and Boards will be found in chapters 7 and 8.

OPERATIONS

The Lloyd's market supplies insurance cover for risks of every kind in the international marine, non-marine, aviation and reinsurance fields, as well as for motor risks in the UK and some other countries. Its capital is provided by the Members (individual and corporate), who make it available to selected syndicates on an annually renewable basis. The business itself is conducted by the syndicate underwriters and management staff, all of whom are employed by the managing agent.

Members

Traditionally the Lloyd's market was founded on Members, whose individual wealth was "the strength behind Lloyd's" and the security of the famed Lloyd's policy. They were exclusively sole traders with, under English law, unlimited personal liability for any losses incurred. However, since 1994 Corporate Membership has been possible and, bringing with it, for the first time in the market's history, membership with limited liability.

Traditionally known as "names", the Members are divided into three functional groups:

- working Members
- external Members
- Corporate Members

Working Members are the underwriters and those Members who work within the

Lloyd's market such as the brokers and agency staff who are Members of, in some cases, their own and usually several other syndicates, and who conduct the daily business of assessing and accepting risks on behalf of the Members. The external Members are, by definition, those Members who have no direct connection with the market through employment. All of the Members of a syndicate carry the risks written by the syndicate in proportion to their participation, irrespective of whether they are working or external names. However, the liability of Corporate Members is different, most significantly because the assets they make available to meet syndicate losses are known and fixed in contrast to the Name with unlimited liability, whose entire wealth is available.

Historically, groups of Members formed syndicates and appointed underwriters to accept risks on their behalf. Today, participation in the Lloyd's market is done through agents and advisers.

Agents and advisers

The activities of both underwriters and individual Members are traditionally managed by agents, of which there are three key types:

● **Members' agent:** advises and administers a Member's Lloyd's affairs (see page 19). This primarily involves selection of suitable syndicates for the Member to participate in and can take the form of a discrete number of specific syndicates, a Bespoke programme, or participation in a much wider pool of syndicates as selected by the agent – a Members' Agent Pooling Arrangement (MAPA). (See page 52.)

● **Managing agent:** responsible for the management of one or more syndicates (see page17).

● **Combined agent:** an agent which combines the responsibilities and activities of a Members' agent and a managing agent – but does so through separate companies.

Unlike individual Members, Corporate Members do not have to appoint a Members' agent. Alternatively, they are able to appoint a Lloyd's adviser to provide syndicate analysis and negotiate syndicate participations (see page 61). Members' agents can and do act as advisers to Corporate Members. Corporate Members may, subject to satisfying appropriate requirements, be their own advisers.

The ownership, control and activities of agents are regulated by the Council of Lloyd's.

Regulation details are available from the Council Secretariat.

Syndicates

An annual venture

These are the main operating units in the Lloyd's market. They have no existence in law and each is in effect an annual venture which ceases to underwrite business at the end of the year, although its books have to remain open for another two to receive claims and establish an accurate assessment of its liabilities (see RITC, page 32). In practice, however, syndicates will continue to operate often for many years with only a few changes to the Members participating in the syndicate.

In any one year as many as two hundred syndicates will be in operation, each one representing a group of Members on behalf of whom an underwriter accepts insurance risk. A Member normally participates in more than one syndicate, both to help spread risk and, logically, to reduce the volatility of results. Both individual and Corporate Members are each responsible only for their own individual liabilities, ie, they have several not joint liability.

Lloyd's brokers

A more powerful form of insurance broking

The unique nature of Lloyd's is reflected in the role of Lloyd's brokers. A Lloyd's broker can obtain cover for policyholders beyond the reach of non-Lloyd's brokers. This is because they have exclusive access to Lloyd's specialist pool of underwriting expertise and short lines of command, both of which create a unique environment in which to structure and place risks. A Lloyd's broker is also especially skilled in constructing policies based on his knowledge of the Lloyd's market, thereby contributing substantially to its effectiveness and responsiveness.

The Lloyd's broker's prime duty is to negotiate the best terms for his clients, the policyholders. To this end he is free to place risks wherever he thinks fit, whether at Lloyd's, with the insurance companies, or both.

The Security of a Lloyd's policy

The cornerstone of a Lloyd's policy's security is the annual audit of underwriters' accounts. The term "audit" can be misleading since the Lloyd's audit is much more than an examination of accounts. It is a searching test of solvency to which every underwriting member's affairs are subjected annually. It is designed to detect any weakness at the earliest possible moment and to ensure that this is remedied and provision made to protect the insured.

The audit is combined with a comprehensive range of additional measures, including the creation and maintenance of special deposits, reserves and funds of last resort. Together they all help to ensure that, as far as possible, a valid Lloyd's policy claim will always eventually be paid.

CHAPTER THREE

The Lloyd's Market in action

A MARKET IN RISK

High returns can mean high risks

Insurance is a risk business and by its nature cyclical. Members can make losses as well as profits. Profits can never be guaranteed and there is no overall prospective average return from membership. Typically, high returns are usually accompanied by high levels of risk. It is inherently difficult to forecast short-term trends or returns in any single year. Not only do underwriting results change but investment income and appreciation are affected by interest rates and investment market performance.

THE SYNDICATE AT WORK

Members have several liability not joint liability

Syndicates are run by a managing agent (see above and chapter 4 page 15) on behalf of all its Members. The agent also employs the syndicate underwriters. Each syndicate tends to specialise in a certain range of business.

Members of syndicates are not in partnership and no Member has joint liability with any other Member of that syndicate for risks underwritten through that syndicate. Members are each individually responsible only for the proportion of each risk written on their behalf.

When a syndicate ceases trading, the obligations of the Members in that syndicate to their existing policyholders remain unaltered. Members cannot resign from a syndicate (or Lloyd's) until all their underwriting commitments have been discharged.

Underwriting limits

Related to solvency requirements

Every year each Member is allowed to underwrite no more than a certain maximum of insurance business premium income (known as the Overall Premium Limit or OPL), the amount being based on the security that Member has deposited with Lloyd's, which in turn is directly related to a prescribed level of Member's solvency. The minimum deposit has varied over the years but in 1994 the minimum deposit requirement was set at £1.5 million for Corporate Members; this was subsequently reduced to £500,000 in 1996. Up to twice that amount may be underwritten, ie £1 million. As long as the right amount of deposit is provided and subject to available capacity there is no upper limit restriction on what a Member may underwrite.

Unlike in 1994 and 1995 there are now no restrictions placed on the proportion of a syndicate allocated capacity which can be provided by Corporate Members either individually or in total. The maximum amount of business or premium income the syndicate is permitted to underwrite is itself limited overall by the aggregate of all the Members' OPLs on that syndicate.

Managing and monitoring

The managing agent must monitor and control premium income earned by its syndicates and is required to take reasonable care to keep the premium income of each of its syndicates within their specified overall capacity.

However, Members have no direct control over whether that part of their OPL allocated to a specific syndicate is exceeded in a particular year of account. This can be due to a number of reasons, such as exchange rate movements', the requirement by the Council that another Member of the syndicate cease underwriting, or from unexpectedly high levels of premium income from coverholders or from reinstatement premiums following a claim on a policy.

Members have no direct control

Maintaining security

The strict and carefully calculated capacity limits set on Members and syndicates and the level of security (ie, deposits) that supports them are crucial to ensuring that Lloyd's is always able to meet the legitimate claims of policyholders and thus uphold its reputation for complete trustworthiness and prompt payment.

Underwriter's responsibilities

The managing agent will allocate a number of underwriters to each of its syndicates. The most senior of these, the Active Underwriter, is responsible to Lloyd's and the syndicate Members for the conduct of all the syndicate's underwriters. Each underwriter, including senior and deputy, has a specific area of expertise.

SETTLEMENT

Premiums and claims balances between syndicates and Lloyd's brokers are handled by Lloyd's Central Accounting. This incorporates features which confer some protection for Members against the risk of the broker becoming insolvent while holding funds due to Lloyd's on the one side or to policyholders on the other.

Generally, claims are accepted or rejected on behalf of a syndicate by the claims manager who reports directly to the Active Underwriter; he does not normally have authority to do so on behalf of any other participating syndicates. Since 1991, however, the latter are generally required to have delegated authority to the Lloyd's Claims Office, which can bind them to follow the leader in respect of claims.

CATEGORIES OF BUSINESS

There are five principal categories of business at Lloyd's:

* marine

* non-marine

* aviation

* motor (predominantly UK)

* term life

In the marine, non-marine, aviation and life markets, both direct insurance and reinsurance is underwritten.

Syndicates'
business
varies

Lloyd's holds a leading position in all these categories, except non-marine. Managing agents often describe the syndicates they manage by reference to the main category in which they have traditionally operated. These categories frequently overlap and can be wider and more varied than their titles suggest. If a syndicate underwrites business in several of the main categories, it is usually referred to as a composite syndicate. Members can expect a more precise outline of the business expected to be underwritten for their syndicate for the following year in the obligatory annual reports and accounts or in their syndicate's business plan.

Short-tail, long-tail, direct and reinsurance business

Every syndicate takes on its own mix of business and risk. This tends to fall into either the "short-tail" category (business in which claims arise and are settled relatively soon after the premium has been paid) or the "long-tail" (in which claims can take many years to materialise and be settled, during which Members can gain from premium investments). Business can also be "direct" (the policyholder has a direct interest in the underlying risk insured) or "reinsurance" (the policyholder is an insurance company or another Lloyd's syndicate).

GEOGRAPHICAL SCOPE

Insurance is one of the most international industries in the world and is subject to a high degree of regulation to protect policyholders. In many countries, it can only be provided by locally-based, licensed insurers. Lloyd's is, however, authorised to underwrite direct business in a number of different countries. At present, well over half of Lloyd's premium income regularly comes from policyholders located abroad, especially North America and Europe. In addition, Lloyd's underwriters underwrite the reinsurance of many insurance companies throughout the world, even in cases where Lloyd's underwriters are unable to underwrite on a direct basis.

More than half of Lloyd's business is non-UK

BUSINESS CYCLE

Although the syndicates are annual ventures, Lloyd's operates a three-year accounting system. This allows the managing agent sufficient time to collect information on known incurred liabilities and also to estimate possible outstanding known and unknown liabilities in order to determine the reinsurance premium required to close the account. If no accurate calculation of liabilities is possible, a year is kept open (see page 32).

Members participate in individual years as well as individual syndicates and all liabilities are calculated in terms of that year and its associated three-year cycle. Moreover, when a year cannot be "closed" and has to remain open beyond the end of the third year, the Member's participation in that year in effect continues until the remaining liabilities have been quantified and reinsured (see page 32).

It is a statutory requirement that each Member be subject to an annual solvency test to demonstrate that, as at the previous 31 December, the Member has sufficient assets at Lloyd's to meet his liabilities.

Annual ventures in a three-year cycle

THE INTRODUCTION OF CORPORATE CAPITAL IN THE LLOYD'S MARKET

Institutional investment was a key element of the Lloyd's business plan issued in April 1993 and which opened up Lloyd's membership to an entirely new type of investor. The Corporate Members are limited liability companies and their shareholders' liability is limited to the extent of the funds invested. Many major US and UK investment banks saw corporate capital at Lloyd's as a major investment opportunity and, within a matter of months, £900 million of capital had been raised to support underwriting activities for the 1994 year of account. This increased yet further for the 1995 account to over £1.2 billion and now nearly 45 per cent of Lloyd's market capacity is supported by corporate capital. The interest shown in investing in this way at Lloyd's stems from the gearing of capital to underwriting capacity which for Corporate Members is 50 per cent or more. Thus not only is the paid-up capital invested but so are the premiums accepted by the underwriting syndicates, thus creating two independent sources of investment return, quite apart from any underwriting profits. In this way, capital invested in Lloyd's corporate vehicles works three times over.

CAPITAL STRUCTURE OF THE MARKET

The traditional syndicate is the only capital structure through which individual Members can participate as sole traders. It is founded upon the annual venture system which, as it implies, means that the capital of the syndicate has to be re-established each year, ie, there is no proper continuity of capital.

The admission of Corporate Members to the market in 1994 effectively changed the ground rules and allowed other capital structures to emerge. In all, 95 Corporate Members commenced trading as limited entities for the 1994 year of account. Of these 95 new incorporated names, 16 were supported by 13 unquoted vehicles and the remaining 79 were backed by 12 quoted investment companies thus constituting a new sub-sector of the FT Actuaries Insurance Index.

Dedicated vehicles

Subsequently, for the 1995 and 1996 accounts there was further expansion of the corporate capital market this time reflecting a change of emphasis in the desired type of corporate vehicle, and favouring the so-called "dedicated" vehicle. This is effectively a Corporate Member promoted to support one or more syndicates of a particular managing agent.

Corporate syndicates

Also introduced for 1995 were "corporate syndicates", which are syndicates consisting of a single Corporate Member. It was envisaged that a corporate syndicate would be operated concurrently and in parallel by the same managing agent and with the same underwriter together with one or more syndicates including individual Members. One of the benefits of a corporate or continuous syndicate is that the syndicate has a single Corporate Member ie, permanent capital and therefore is an alternative structure to the annual venture system.

Independent corporate syndicates

An extension of this principle was approved for the 1996 year of account. This is described as an independent corporate syndicate which, as the terminology implies, is independent of any existing syndicate. However, any application to establish such a syndicate will be subject to final approval by Lloyd's.

Common ownership

The introduction of this type of syndicate for 1995 provoked considerable interest, prompting investors to consider acquiring a share in the managing agency which ran the existing syndicates. Initially, the rules precluded acquisition of a shareholding of more than 25%. However, this barrier has been lifted and, subject to satisfying a number of different requirements, it is now possible for a Corporate Member (a so-called aligned Member) to acquire 100% shareholding in a managing agent.

Integrated Lloyd's vehicles

A further stage in the development of the continuous syndicate would be for the capital provider and the managing agency to be integrated in a single structure. For technical reasons, they might be housed in separate legal entities but those entities would be under common ownership of control. The management would then have a greater certainty as to the continued provisions of the regulatory capital to support the business. It is just this type of development that has recently been approved by Lloyd's. These are known as integrated Lloyd's vehicles or ILVs.

Such vehicles would in many respects be similar to an insurance company, the one significant difference being that the regulatory capital would be held by Lloyd's as Funds at Lloyd's, rather than internally as is the case with an insurance company. It would be required to meet Lloyd's regulatory standards and would be able to trade in the UK and some other countries under Lloyd's licence.

Insurance carriers

Insurance carriers already in existence which operate outside the Lloyd's market will be allowed to acquire control of a managing agent and Corporate Members. However, this will only be possible in the case of managing agents if the carrier also has a substantial interest in the Corporate Member which, in turn, has a significant participation on each of the syndicates managed by that managing agent. In order to gain approval, a number of other requirements will have to be met, including certain undertakings and guarantees.

CHAPTER FOUR

The Lloyd's Market in action
KEY ROLES AND PROCEDURES IN DETAIL

SYNDICATE OPERATION - MEMBERS & THEIR MANAGING AGENTS

As the result of the publication of the Value Report, many of the rights and obligations of Members and agents, in particular the rights of Members, have been strengthened.

Authorisation of managing agents

To confer the necessary authorisation on the managing agent a separate agency agreement is required between the syndicate Member and the agent. However, in the normal course of events, the managing agent will not deal directly with the Member, but with the Member's agent or, in the case of Corporate Members, the Lloyd's adviser will act as intermediary.

Independence of managing agents

Although the relationship between Member and managing agent is one of principal and agent, until recently the Member could not insist on maintaining participation in a syndicate. Since the beginning of 1995 Members now have the right to maintain their participation in a syndicate. Members also have the right to participate in any future increase of the underwriting capacity of the syndicate. An agent cannot be forced to act for a principal if he does not wish it. However, the managing agent's ability to give notice of termination to a Member is subject to restrictions contained in the standard agency agreement or is imposed by the Council.

Termination

A Member may terminate an agreement with a managing agent by giving written notice by 31 August in any year (in limited circumstances, by a later date), thus discontinuing participation in any affected syndicate for subsequent years of account. If a managing agent gives notice of termination to a Member, the Member may appeal to the Council (see also MAPA regulations, page 52).

Notice of termination

A period of notice must be given by the managing agent when terminating the agency (and hence the Member's membership of the affected syndicates); in 1994, for example, this had to take place by 31 May for effective termination on 31 December of the same year in relation to future years. From 1995, such notice of termination will first have to be approved by the Council.

Non-transferable participation

At the time of writing, syndicate participation cannot be assigned during or at the end of a year, nor can an existing Member require the managing agent to accept a third party as a Member in his place (other than in the case of conversion).

Capacity allocation by auction

The concept of a system by which value for syndicate participations could be achieved was first outlined in Lloyd's Task Force Report in 1992. Recent work on this idea has finally culminated in the establishment of an auction system. This involved a series of four weekly public auctions during August 1995 (since then the period has been extended). Under this system any individual or Corporate Member currently underwriting can either tender (sell) some or all of their syndicate participations or alternatively subscribe (buy) for additional or new syndicate participations.

The auction process largely replaces the system of syndicate capacity allocation which took place during the latter part of the year and for no consideration.

It is entirely possible that should the auction system be successful it could evolve to the extent that it will be ultimately the only method by which syndicate capacity can be acquired or relinquished.

Limits to the Society's power

The Society has no power to secure the continued participation of a particular active underwriter or other directors, officers or employees of a managing agent.

THE WORK OF THE MANAGING AGENT

Note: the following will provide an additional insight into the functioning of a typical syndicate.

The role and duties of the managing agent

In principle, these are:
- to determine underwriting policy and to make arrangements for the underwriting of risks;
- to appoint and supervise one or more individuals to be the active underwriters for each syndicate under the agent's control.

In addition, the managing agent is expected to approve and supervise arrangements for:
- the acceptance and pricing of the risks to be underwritten by the active underwriters; the receipt of the premiums agreed with brokers;
- the agreement and settlement of claims made against a syndicate;
- the negotiation and management of a syndicate's reinsurances;
- the management of the investments held in the Sterling, US$ and Canadian $ Premiums Trust Funds;
- the management and control of a syndicate's expenses;
- monitoring and controlling the income underwritten by the syndicate and taking reasonable steps to ensure that Members' syndicate premium limits are not exceeded;
- the maintenance of accounting records and statistical data for the syndicate and the preparation and audit of a syndicate's accounts;
- distribution of profits and, where necessary, making cash calls on Members to provide for underwriting losses;
- compliance with relevant domestic and overseas taxation and legislative requirements;
- the approval of the premium for, and effecting, the reinsurance required to close each year of account.

The managing agent's discretion

- The managing agent (through the active underwriter) has absolute discretion in the selection of the risks to be underwritten on behalf of a Member.

Managing agents carry key responsibilities

- Any change in the agent's role which might vary from the standard form of agreement between an agent and Member has to be approved by the Council, with the exception of matters concerning:
  - fees and commissions (in which the agent has greater discretion)
  - reinsurance to close (RITC, see page 48) of the liabilities associated with policies allocated to the 1985 account or before (in which the agent has no discretion).
- While under the agency agreement, the managing agent must give notice in the syndicate's business plan of the general nature of business expected to be written in the year of the report and in the year following. The agent nevertheless has discretion to write other types of business if he is satisfied that it is in a syndicate's interest. However, the agent is required to write to the Members promptly, informing them of any subsequent material change to the business plan.
- Managing agents are not required to take out errors-and-omissions insurance cover, although it remains recommended best practice.

Syndicate voting controls

Certain kinds of major decisions by a managing agent can affect the nature and existence of a syndicate. Some of these are already covered by the standard agent/Member agreement, in which they are subject to prior approval by a meeting of the syndicate. Managing agents must now give names prior notice of the following:

- Merger
- Sale of business
- Ceasing to trade

It is likewise proposed that Members representing a specified proportion of a syndicate's capacity should be entitled to request the Council to transfer the management of a syndicate to another managing agent.

Regulation of managing agents

The ownership, control and scope of activities of managing agents are closely regulated by the Council. Such regulation covers, amongst others, fitness for the task, participation by directors/partners in the syndicate as Members, conflicts of interest, disclosure and reporting.

Comprehensive details are obtainable from the Council Secretariat.

REMUNERATION OF MANAGING AGENTS

Fees and profit commission

Managing agents charge management fees and profit commission to Members underwriting on their syndicates. The fee is usually a percentage of the Member's syndicate premium limit; and the commission a percentage of the underwriting profit earned by the Member as a result of his participation in the syndicate, as well as of the investment income and capital appreciation arising on that part of the Member's Premiums Trust Funds under the control of the managing agent. The basis on which profit commission is calculated is standard for all the syndicates but the rate of commission is freely negotiable. For years of account after 1992 the commission takes into account the syndicate's losses, if any, in the preceding two years.

Managing agent's commission reflects losses as well as profits

Published rates and Council prescription

The Council has the power to review remuneration and to prescribe maximum levels of managing agents' fees and to regulate the basis on which commission is charged. However, managing agents are free to negotiate the rate of their remuneration individually with each syndicate Member subject to them being published in the register of charges open for inspection by all Members.

Expenses

Managing agents are also entitled to charge appropriate and reasonable expenses. These are normally deducted from the Members' Premiums Trust Funds. Syndicate expenses other than these are the subject of a code of practice issued by the Council and reviewed by each syndicate's auditors at each year end.

MEMBERS' AGENTS

Members' agents always act on behalf of individual Members in the Lloyd's market; Corporate Members generally participate through Lloyd's advisers, unless they wish to join a MAPA (see page 52), in which case they, too, must appoint a Members' agent. Members' agents can and do act also as Lloyd's advisers.

Selecting a Members' agent

It is critical to select the right Members' agent. There are a number of different types of Members' agent (see below). Before concluding an agency agreement with a Member, every Members' agent is required to provide written information about itself, either in a standard form Members' Agent's Information Report (MAIR) available from Lloyd's Market Information Centre or in its own brochure. However, the information thus provided is no substitute for first-hand discussion between a prospective Member and a Members' agent.

Types of Members' agent

There are a number of different types of Members' agent, including:

- Independent Members' agent. These have no association with any managing agency or Lloyd's broker and pride themselves on the independence of their advice.
- Members' agents associated with Lloyd's brokers. In addition to being independent of managing agents, these agents may have more numerous contacts in the underwriting community.
- Combined agents. With direct access to their own managed syndicates, combined agents may be in a better position to offer places to Members; however, *the independence of their views cannot be taken for granted.*

Multiple Members' agent

A Member may have as many Members' agents as required with one acting as overall co-ordinating agent, although most have only one.

The Members' agents' role

- To recommend which syndicates to join, with the aim of creating a balanced spread of business on syndicates in the four main markets of Lloyd's, in accordance with the Members' wishes.

- To review the syndicates which the Members' agent supports and to make recommendations about any changes to that participation. The Members' agent may recommend withdrawing all of its Members from a particular syndicate. However, such a decision would not be binding on the Members so affected, as they retain the right of participation against the recommendation of their agent.

- To act for members wishing to buy or sell syndicate participations at auction.

- To negotiate for capacity with syndicates' managing agents.

  The bases for fees and commission for these and the Members' agents' other services are provided for in the standard agency agreements.

- In certain cases, to offer additional services to Members, such as tax and investment advice (through authorised companies) in respect of underwriting funds. Charges for these services would be agreed independently of the normal fees.

LLOYD'S ADVISERS (CORPORATE MEMBERS ONLY)

The Corporate Member does not have to appoint a Members' agent. However, unless the Society agrees otherwise, it is obliged to appoint a Lloyd's adviser to provide syndicate analysis and negotiate syndicate participations.

The Lloyd's adviser will have no general authority to commit a Member to a particular syndicate; the final decision rests with the Member.

The Lloyd's adviser must be appointed under written terms of business; the Member is free to negotiate these with the adviser. If circumstances require it, the Council has the power to prescribe mandatory terms and conditions.

CHAPTER FIVE

The Lloyd's Market in action

KEEPING ACCOUNTS

The accounting aspects of underwriting at Lloyd's are characterised by a number of unique features, of which the most notable are those relating to:

Overall Operation
● The three-year accounting system
● The year of account
● Capacity

Members
● The overall premium limit (OPL)
● Funds at Lloyd's
● Premiums Trust Funds
● Reinsurance to close (RITC)
● Run-off accounts
● Cash calls

THE THREE-YEAR ACCOUNTING SYSTEM

Accuracy and reliability determine three-year accounting system

While this system is said to have its origins in Lloyd's early marine market "voyage accounting", research shows that in the types of insurance business in which Lloyd's is most active today it is common to keep a year of account open for three years to allow a reasonable period of time to elapse in which to allow premiums to be received and for claims arising from business underwritten in that trading year to be notified and settled. The result is to enable a fair judgement of the likely profit or loss on that year of account. The distribution of profits, whether from underwriting itself or from investments held in the Premiums Trust Funds (see page 30), does not take place until after the end of the third year. Furthermore, that distribution is not permitted before the year of account on which the three-year period is based has been "closed" by way of reinsurance, the so-called Reinsurance to Close (RITC – see page 32).

However, in the insurance company market (which does not operate the Annual Venture system requiring the equitable transfer of liabilities and reserves between each syndicate year of account) one-year accounting is the norm.

Recent efforts to explore the possibility of shortening the three-year accounting cycle and introduce two-year accounting encountered major regulatory barriers, especially in relation to the European Union Insurance accounts directive. However, a move to annual accounting would bring Lloyd's into line with the main provisions of this directive. Such a move is now actively under consideration.

THE YEAR OF ACCOUNT

Risk allocation

For the purposes of accounting, every risk accepted has to be allocated to its specific year of account. This is known as "closing". Up to 1995, the year is determined by the date on which the broker who placed the risk first submits the relevant documentation to the Lloyd's Policy Signing Office; all subsequent transactions (eg, endorsements or additional premiums) relating to that risk are then allocated to that same year. This can, in practice, mean that the period of cover differs from the year of account. *1995: inception date allocation*

During 1995, a new system known as "inception date allocation" came into effect. Under this approach, risks underwritten are generally allocated to the year of account in which the period of cover commences.

Binding authorities

Risks written by coverholders under binding authorities are allocated to the year of account in which the binding authority is granted, irrespective of when the coverholder accepts the risks. However, some risks are underwritten by syndicates which are no longer underwriting in the year of account in which the policy associated with that risk was issued. Such risks are therefore allocated to the year of account in which the risk was accepted or, alternatively, an earlier year in which the syndicate was still underwriting. As a result, Members of a syndicate for a particular year of account may be underwriting business actually transacted before or after the calendar year in which the business is accounted for.

Capacity

a) Capacity management

Capacity management and capital allocation are keys to policyholder security and the profitability of the market

One of the lessons of the late 1980s was that uncontrolled expansion of capacity can lead to undesirable concentrations which endanger policyholder security and expose Members to unacceptable levels of risk. A system has been introduced for reviewing significant capacity increases proposed by managing agents. In addition, if the Council concludes that there are excessive concentrations of capacity in a particular class of business, the premium limits for syndicates underwriting this business will be adjusted. Further measures of control include syndicate voting rights (see page 18) and risk weighting of capital (see page 28).

b) Qualifying quota share arrangement

Since 1992, syndicates have been permitted to write business up to a specified limit (20% in 1995) above their allocated capacity through "qualifying quota share reinsurance arrangements" placed with qualifying reinsurers of all classes of businesses. The associated premiums can be deducted from the gross premiums prior to measuring receipts against the syndicate's overall allocated capacity.

A qualifying arrangement must be for a fixed percentage of income in respect of all business within a specified category or categories. Such category or categories in aggregate must represent at least 15% of a syndicate's allocated capacity, by reference to the syndicate's business plan, although this may constitute several different Lloyd's risk categories. The maximum percentage which can be ceded under each quota share arrangement in relation to each specific category of business that will qualify for premium limit relief will be 50%, subject to the overall restriction of 20% of the total syndicate allocated capacity.

To the extent that such a quota share reinsurance is placed with non-Lloyd's insurers, syndicates will be required to pay a contribution to the Central Fund of 1.5% of premiums receivable in excess of what their allocated capacity would have been but for the qualifying quota share.

c) Pre-emption

Beginning with capacity increases for the 1995 underwriting year, any proposed increases in a syndicate's capacity must be offered on a pro rata basis to the existing Members.

Any capacity arising from pre-emption rights not taken up (and from deaths or resignations of Members) can be offered by the managing agent to any Members' agent or Corporate Member it chooses (subject to the limits in force on corporate participation in syndicates). See also MAPA (page 52).

THE OVERALL PREMIUM LIMIT (OPL)

A measure of underwriting capacity

Premiums are the economic price the free market puts on a specific risk; they can therefore be regarded as a good measure of such a risk. In general, underwriting risk is consequently regulated by reference to premium income; the underwriting capacity of each Member of Lloyd's is thus fixed as a maximum amount of premium income (in other words, a particular degree of risk) which may be accepted by the Member for any year of account – whence the term "overall premium limit" or OPL.

Premiums are a measure of risk

Maintaining balance

A Member's OPL in respect of each year of account must not exceed the multiple prescribed by the Council of the Member's funds at Lloyd's (see next page). To avoid unbalanced and needlessly risky concentrations, a Corporate Member's OPL for a year of account will be apportioned prior to the start of each year amongst the syndicates to which the Member, in consultation with the syndicates' managing agents through the Lloyd's adviser, has agreed to belong. The limits to any concentration may vary from time to time; in 1994 no more than 20% of a Corporate Member's OPL could be allocated to a single syndicate. Other restrictions were placed on the proportion of syndicate capacity which could be provided by Corporate Members, either individually or in total.

Spreading risk

However, the Lloyd's Regulatory Board recently approved the lifting of all these restrictions for 1996 in anticipation of the introduction of risk based capital requirements.

Termination of syndicate membership by *force majeure*

If the Member's agent's appointment as agent of a Member of the syndicate is terminated during a year of account because the Member dies or becomes insolvent or the agreement is terminated by force of law, liability for risks and syndicate expenses is terminated and entitlements to premiums are calculated as if the Member had not belonged to the syndicate for that year of account.

Termination of syndicate membership due to suspension or act of omission

If a Member is suspended from underwriting for any reason other than disciplinary, or if the managing agent terminates its agency because the Member has failed to pay a cash call, termination is determined and calculated as if the year of account had come to an end on the day of the Member's suspension and the syndicate had re-formed without the Member on the following day.

FUNDS AT LLOYD'S

Members' security

The Members' commitment to security for the policyholder
In the interests of protecting Lloyd's ultimate ability to meet claims in the event of a Member's insolvency, Lloyd's requires each Member of the syndicate to provide security equal to a specified proportion of the Member's Overall Premium Limit. This security (whose form the Council may prescribe and which is additional to the amounts held under the control of managing agents in the Sterling, US$ and Canadian $ Premiums Trust Funds) will include the Member's Lloyd's deposit and additional reserve funds. The total amount is known as the Member's "funds at Lloyd's". The minimum required level of such funds is reviewed and monitored for compliance by the Council before the commencement of each year of account; the Member must ensure that the level specified is maintained continuously throughout the year.

Shortfalls in funds at Lloyd's

Three factors can cause Members' funds at Lloyd's to fall below the required minimum:

● reductions in the value of the assets in the Lloyd's deposit and other funds at Lloyd's;
● the Member's OPL is exceeded;

● underwriting losses or deficiencies have to be made good.

The importance attached to correcting any such shortfalls entail the Council possessing wide powers to take the necessary action, including requiring the Member to provide additional funds prior to giving permission for continuation of underwriting.

Monitoring and valuation

The overall monitoring process of the Member's funds primarily involves valuing them (for the Member's solvency) as at 31 December in each year. If any deficiency at that date has not been made good prior to 31 October in the following year, then the Member's OPL will be reduced for the next year of account.

Additional risk/fund balance measures

A number of additional procedures and interventions also play an important part in ensuring that a Member's funding is safely matched with the risks accepted through syndicate underwriting, as follows:

Matching funding to risk

● If at any time the Member's funds fall 15% below the latest valuation, the Member must notify Lloyd's. The Council will respond as required, including directing that the Member's overall level of underwriting business at Lloyd's be reduced.

● If the Member's OPL has been exceeded, the Council may require the Member to reduce the level of future underwriting business – without permitting a corresponding reduction in the level of funds at Lloyd's – until the Council is satisfied that the effects of overwriting have been sufficiently compensated for.

● If there are any outstanding amounts to be paid by the Member to meet liabilities on open years (years of account that have not yet been closed) or in respect of closed year losses, the Member's OPL and underwriting capacity will be reduced in proportion to the funds at Lloyd's available to that Member.

Financial pressures on Members in early years

A new Lloyd's Member will receive no profits from syndicate participation until, at the earliest, the middle of the fourth year after the Member begins accepting risks.

Testing Member solvency and asset adequacy

Throughout the period before any profits are distributed, the Member's solvency position will continue to be calculated at each year end (see Solvency Testing, page 45) to ensure that the Member's assets will meet liabilities, either as estimated by the managing agent or on the basis of reserving percentages as prescribed by the Department of Trade and Industry. These percentages cannot take account of differences in the profitability of particular syndicates.

Relieving pressures on a Member's assets

Additional Member assets are often required in the early years

As a result of these delays and possible cash calls, should a syndicate unexpectedly run short of funds, a Member's initial funds at Lloyd's (and hence the OPL) can come under pressure during this period, especially if business has been underwritten which is near the limit of the Member's capacity. It is therefore advisable for prospective Members to confer with their Member's agent or Lloyd's adviser(s) and potential syndicate managing agents to establish whether it would be advisable to retain additional assets to enable their funds at Lloyd's to be supplemented if necessary. They will in any event have to retain assets to meet demands which cannot be paid out of their Premiums Trust Funds or funds at Lloyd's.

Refinements planned for funds at Lloyd's (risk-based capital)

Refinements of the funds at Lloyd's system are under consideration; these will introduce risk-based weightings reflecting the different lines of business underwritten by individual syndicates.

The original proposal for risk-weighted capital formed part of the recommendation of the Walker Report (June 1992) on syndicate participations and the LMX Spiral. The Value Group Report (May 1994) stated that it was the Council's (of Lloyd's) intention to introduce risk-weighted capital for the 1996 underwriting year. This target date was not met. However, a consultative document was issued to the Market in August 1995 as a result of which a system has now been introduced for 1997.

The proposals operate at capital provider level with each class of business being underwritten having attributed to it a capital requirement based on a predetermined formula. It is designed to encourage capital providers to underwrite a broad spread of classes of business across a number of different underwriters and managing agents, thereby managing class of business, underwriter and management risk. A system of credits will be applied which will acknowledge diversity in these areas.

It follows that underwriting programmes that concentrate on only a few classes and underwriters and managing agents will require more capital support than those that are broadly spread. It is intended that this system will have the effect of enhancing the protection afforded to policyholders.

Income distribution and management

Interest, other investment income and realised capital profits arising from cash or other assets deposited may be distributed to the Member, less applicable taxes, but will be subject to the requirements of the Deposit Trust Deed. Within permitted investment criteria and, again, subject to the safeguards contained in the Deeds, Members may nominate an appropriately authorised person to manage assets held under their Deeds. Where the Council agrees, such management may include foreign exchange hedging arrangements.

Release of funds at Lloyd's

Following a reduction in OPL, a Member may apply for the release of part of the funds at Lloyd's only if:

- an amount is retained equal to the funds at Lloyd's requirement for the highest OPL of the last three years;
- there are no "earmarkings" of any kind;
- the Member does not participate in any syndicates in run-off.

Such releases are not normally allowed while the annual solvency test is under way.

PREMIUMS TRUST FUNDS

Payment and security vehicle

*A repository
for premiums*

Claims and underwriting expenses are borne by the Member through the Sterling, US$ and Canadian $ Premiums Trust Funds (PTF); these are the repository of all the premiums received on the Member's behalf, as well as of investment return on PTF assets and cash calls paid by the Member.

Although Members each have their own discrete PTF (including American and Canadian Trust Funds – see page 32), and although the funds thus held are available to meet exclusively that Member's liabilities, the operation of PTFs in general occurs on a co-mingled basis, usually grouped by syndicate or, in certain cases, by managing agent. This may mean that a Member's PTF monies can, in effect, be on loan to other Members (on the same or another syndicate) to meet their underwriting liabilities for a current or previous year of account. Although such loans have in practice been supported by the Central Fund, Members whose PTF assets are used in this way are incurring a credit risk. Since loan policy is determined by the managing agent, the prospective Member should make inquiries before a decision is made to join a particular syndicate. The Council does not directly monitor compliance with the terms of the relevant trust deeds, although they are reviewed regularly by syndicate auditors in their report on the annual syndicate return.

*When PTF
assets are
functioning
as loans,
Members
are incurring
a technical
credit risk*

Taking profits

*No profits
before
fulfilling
obligations
to the
policyholder*

Profits in respect of a particular year's underwriting on a syndicate will not normally be released to the Member until the relevant year has been closed by reinsurance-to-close and the Society has confirmed the Member's overall underwriting position as solvent.

All profits due to a Member from profitable syndicates are transferred to that part of the Member's PTFs under the control of the Member's agent. However, before any accumulated funds can be released to the Member, they must first be used by the agent to:

● meet any cash calls to be paid by the Member to any unprofitable syndicates in which the Member participated through that agent; and to

● establish reserves to meet possible liabilities from underwriting in other years of account or on other syndicates.

● The Council intends that, for OPL purposes, it will eventually become possible for Members to treat these reserves as part of their funds at Lloyd's, subject to appropriate safeguards.

Constraints on unclosed years of account

When a year of account remains open (a year which a syndicate has been unable to close in the normal way because it still carries unquantifiable liabilities), the Member participating in that year will not be allowed access to any apparent surplus of funds derived from that year of account of the syndicate.

If there is any doubt about the adequacy of reserves in a Member's PTF and funds at Lloyd's to meet all that Member's Lloyd's liabilities, the Society will not allow the release of profits to the Member.

Assets held in PTFs are not available to a Member's general creditors, nor does a managing agent or a Member's agent have any right to them; thus the insolvency of either the Member or agents does not affect the availability of funds in the PTFs to meet outstanding underwriting claims.

PTF Trustees

The trustees of a Member's PTF will be individuals appointed by each of the Member's managing agents, by Lloyd's itself and, in some cases, by individuals appointed by Lloyd's. The relevant managing agent(s) have the power to direct the trustees appointed by them to invest the trust funds within a range of investments prescribed by the Council and to delegate investment management to an appropriately authorised person. By agreement with any of their managing agents, Members may nominate a person or persons (who may be connected with the Member or Members) to be the investment manager for a proportion or all of the PTFs of the relevant syndicate or syndicates.

Ultimate control of PTF assets remains with the trustee

However, the custody and ultimate control over such assets must remain with the trustee, in accordance with the terms of the Premiums Trust Deed. Furthermore, the investment performance of the nominated investment manager will be to the benefit of the syndicate as a whole rather than of trust funds of the nominating Member.

Non-UK underwriting

The Premium Trust Deed provides for separate treatment of overseas underwriting business through Lloyd's American Trust Funds (ATFs) and Canadian Trust Funds (CTFs). These trust funds receive the premiums on US or Canadian dollar policies issued in any country by Lloyd's Members, and pay any losses, claims, returns or premiums, reinsurance premiums and other outgoings connected with the Member's American or Canadian dollar business respectively (including expenses and remuneration of the trustees and the salary, commission or other remuneration of agents employed in that business).

REINSURANCE-TO-CLOSE (RITC)

Closing
a year of
account

By the end of a year of account, a syndicate will have accumulated a number of outstanding liabilities, actual, estimated and carried over from earlier years of account. The Members remain severally responsible for them and, until they are dealt with, the year of account cannot be closed and neither can its profits be released. The usual solution is to reinsure the liabilities, without limit in time or amount, and re-allocate them to the following year of account of the same syndicate. Reinsurance takes effect when the Members have paid a premium commensurate with the total outstanding liabilities for the year in question, including liabilities from previous years and those incurred but not yet reported ("IBNR"). Such payment entitles the Members not only to any benefit arising from reinsurance but also to other recoveries relating to the same risks and, in addition, all other rights arising out of the original underwriting of those risks.

RITC is a reinsurance contract for whose arrangement the managing agent has absolute discretion on behalf of both the reinsured and the reinsuring syndicate(s); no Member or group can either approve or veto it. It is, however, subject to scrutiny by auditors who must comment on its reasonableness. The operation of RITC has a number of restrictions placed on it, pre-1993 and post-1994.

OPEN YEAR ACCOUNTS

An open year account is a year of account which has not been closed by RITC (see above). This usually relates to the first two years of the three-year accounting cycle.

However, a year of account may remain open even after the end of the third year. This *Containing* may happen for a number of reasons, but is usually the result of uncertainty in quanti- *uncertainty* fying existing liabilities. This makes it difficult to fix a premium which is fair to both the reinsured and the reinsuring Members. In these circumstances closure may take a number of years during which no Members' funds or profits can be released unless authorised by the Council.

A year of account that is left open after the third year is referred to as a run-off year of account and has the effect of isolating the liabilities of that syndicate year; they will not be carried forward to Members underwriting in subsequent years during the time in which the year remains open.

All claims for the run-off year of account will be met by Members of that syndicate year of account.

The managing agent must prepare a report explaining why the year has been left open. If required, the agent must also commission a report from an independent auditor; this will include a report on the agent's report. A decision to leave a year open has to be communicated to all relevant Members' agents and Lloyd's advisers as soon as possible and a syndicate meeting convened by the agent to allow them to examine the reasons for it.

In certain circumstances, special reinsurance arrangements are possible for either the syndicate or personally for individual Members whose syndicates cannot close a year by RITC in the usual way. These are available from CentreWrite, the insurance company wholly owned by the Society.

RUN-OFF

A syndicate is regarded as being in run-off when it ceases to trade. The effect on the Members is similar to a year of account being kept open, ie, no profits can be distributed until all the liabilities are settled for that syndicate for each underwriting year of account. A syndicate in run-off is not permitted to underwrite any new business.

CASH CALLS

Cash calls are another element in the range of measures imposed by Lloyd's to ensure that policyholders are protected. The managing agent is obliged to make calls for cash from Members if a syndicate makes an audited loss in a closed year of account or if

Cash calls have priority there is a deficiency attributable to a syndicate in run-off (including expenses or commissions) or, sometimes, to an open year (a year of account which has yet to reach its allotted closure date).

Cash calls must be paid irrespective of any claim which the Member may have against a managing agent. If the agent has to borrow money to pay claims, the cost may be passed on to the Member; and if a Member fails to meet a cash call, the Council can insist that the Member's funds at Lloyd's should be used. If these funds are not subsequently replenished, the Member will ultimately be required to reduce underwriting or cease it altogether.

CHAPTER SIX

Performance, Profit and Prospects

It is worth repeating that insurance is a risk business and by its nature cyclical; Members can experience losses as well as profits. It is also worth repeating that profits can never be guaranteed and it is not possible to forecast an overall prospective average return to a Member from their membership; typically, high returns are usually accompanied by high levels of risk.

No guarantee of profits

In the Lloyd's business plan, Planning for Profit, published in April 1993, a target was set of a pre-tax return of 10% on capacity over the underwriting cycle.

The table below illustrates a 10% pre-tax return on overall premium limit coupled with an assumed 7% investment return, ultimately expressed as a return on capital invested.

Target Pre-Tax Return ~ % Per Annum

	Individual Names	Incorporated Names
Profit/OPL	10	10
Solvency	30	50
Return of Funds at Lloyd's	33	20
Interest on Investment Funds	7	7
Return on capital	40	27

The chart overleaf shows the profit record of the Lloyd's market from 1971. The period 1988-92 shows the combined effects of excess capacity, weak rating environment and a high frequency of catastrophe losses. Since then capacity has reduced and the rating environment has strengthened significantly. The structure of catastrophe reinsurance has also not changed significantly during that period. *Source: Lloyd's Closed Year Results.*

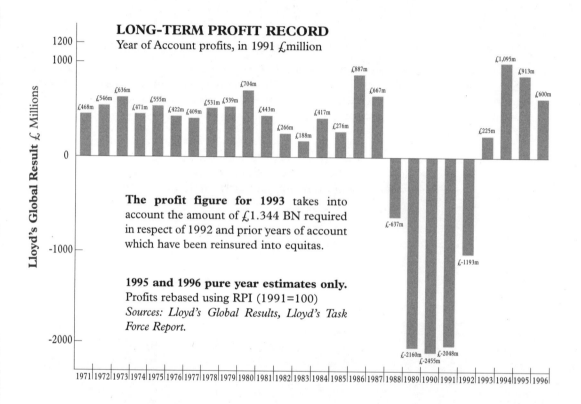

LONG-TERM PROFIT RECORD
Year of Account profits, in 1991 £million

Lloyd's Global Result £ Millions

£468m £546m £636m £471m £555m £422m £409m £531m £539m £704m £443m £266m £188m £417m £276m £887m £667m £-637m £-2160m £-2455m £-1193m £-2048m £225m £1,095m £913m £600m

The profit figure for 1993 takes into account the amount of £1.344 BN required in respect of 1992 and prior years of account which have been reinsured into equitas.

1995 and 1996 pure year estimates only.
Profits rebased using RPI (1991=100)
Sources: Lloyd's Global Results, Lloyd's Task Force Report.

1971 1972 1973 1974 1975 1976 1977 1978 1979 1980 1981 1982 1983 1984 1985 1986 1987 1988 1989 1990 1991 1992 1993 1994 1995 1996

Recognising the problems caused by the excess capacity in the late 1980s, Lloyd's intends to manage changes in its capital base for; this may include a price mechanism under which those providing the additional capacity may be required to make additional contributions to Lloyd's. Limits may be set in relation to the market as a whole or in relation to different classes of business.

CHAPTER SEVEN

The framework of security

GOVERNANCE

For the holders of insurance policies, Lloyd's is another word for security. That security with all its meanings and force is necessarily woven into the very fabric of the organisation and over three centuries has been repeatedly adjusted and strengthened to meet the challenges of the constantly changing business environment.

The Society of Lloyd's

 The first official steps to formalise Lloyd's security was the 1871 Act of Parliament, which caused the Members of the Lloyd's underwriting community to be united into a Society.

The Society, both itself and through subsidiaries, today provides a wide range of facilities and support services for the benefit of the Members, including the premises in which Lloyd's business takes place. Together with their permanent staff, these facilities and services are colloquially known as the "Corporation of Lloyd's". Headed by a Chief Executive Officer, the Corporation assists Lloyd's Council and Boards.

The Corporation of Lloyd's

The Council is a much more recent creation, having been established by the Lloyd's Act of 1982. It has ultimate overall responsibility for, and control of, the affairs of the Society, including rule-making, market discipline and the conduct of business at Lloyd's.

The Council of Lloyd's

To further strengthen central regulatory powers in the light of the losses experienced by a number of Lloyd's syndicates in the late '80s and early '90s, two Boards were set up at the beginning of 1993: the Lloyd's Market Board (which advances the interests of Lloyd's); and the Lloyd's Regulatory Board (which protects policyholders and Members).

The Market Board and the Regulatory Board

The majority of the Council's functions have been devolved to the Boards.

THE COUNCIL OF LLOYD'S

Rule-making and disciplinary powers are vested in the Council by the Lloyd's Act of 1982. Since the Boards were set up, the Council has retained: the exclusive power to make bye-laws; to take decisions on certain other specific matters; the responsibility and the power to review the performance of the Boards; and to revoke or vary their powers.

Rule-making and disciplinary powers

Composition

Under the Act, the Council must comprise working Lloyd's Members, external Members and nominated Council members. No more than two-thirds of the Council may be working Lloyd's Members. From 1 January 1995 it will consist of:

6 working Members
6 external Members (including one representing Corporate Members)
6 nominated Members

Working Members are elected from and by other working Members only and normally hold office for three years. External Members are elected by other external Members, both individual and corporate, and normally hold office for four years. Nominated Members are appointed by the Council and subject to confirmation by the Governor of the Bank of England; their tenure generally lasts three years.

The Council elects from amongst its working Members the Chairman of Lloyd's and two or more Deputy Chairmen. One of the nominated Members of the Council is the Chief Executive Officer of the Society and Corporation.

THE MARKET BOARD

Advancing the interests of Lloyd's

Chaired by the Chairman of Lloyd's and with sixteen members, comprising underwriters, brokers and corporation staff, the Lloyd's Market Board is charged with advancing the commercial interest of the society and co-ordinating and leading dealings with governments, the media and other outside bodies. It is responsible for the strategy to advance Lloyd's competitiveness and for the provision of cost-effective central services. It also sets minimum standards in areas affecting the reputation, efficiency and cost-effectiveness of the market.

THE REGULATORY BOARD

Advancing the interest of the policyholder

The Board has sixteen members (four nominated and five external members of the Council; four working members of the Society and the Director, Regulatory Division. It is responsible for establishing and enforcing rules for regulation of the Lloyd's market as well as agreeing standards of conduct applying to all types of businesses trading at Lloyd's. The rules are designed to ensure compliance with legal requirements, the protection of policyholders and of the interests of Lloyd's Members and their agents. The Board also oversees the Council's disciplinary functions.

BYE-LAWS

Bye-laws must be made, revoked or amended by a special resolution of the Council, which requires separate majority votes both of the working members and of all other members of the Council.

GOVERNING LAW

With certain limited exceptions, all the agreements and deeds entered into by Members of the Society and their managing agents and Lloyd's trustees are governed by English law. Members are required to submit to the exclusive jurisdiction of the English courts in respect of any dispute arising under the law. Lloyd's US and Canadian Trust Deeds are exempt from this ordinance.

CHAPTER EIGHT

The Framework of Security

REGULATION

EXTERNAL REGULATION IN THE UK

The Insurance Companies Act 1982

The powers of the Insurance Companies Act 1982 (ICA) are exercised on behalf of the Secretary of State for Trade and Industry by the Department of Trade and Industry (DTI). The Act has detailed provisions regarding insurance companies' minimum solvency ratios and annual returns to be made to the DTI.

Because of the regulatory regime provided by the Lloyd's Acts, most of the ICA's requirements do not apply to Members of Lloyd's. However, the following are required of Lloyd's:

- All premiums must be paid into Premium Trust Funds;
- Accounts must be prepared and audited annually and a certificate of solvency of each underwriting Member delivered to the DTI;
- The Council must file an annual return summarising the extent and character of the insurance business done by the Members of Lloyd's.

Solvency regulation in the UK

In addition, the ICA requires the Members of Lloyd's taken together to maintain a minimum margin of solvency.

To demonstrate compliance, the Statutory Statement of Business (SSOB) which the Council is required to deposit each year with the Secretary of State includes a "Statement of Solvency" based on the aggregated assets and liabilities of the Members of Lloyd's taken as a whole, as at the end of the year of account preceding the deposit of the SSOB.

Assets are taken to include:

- each Member's funds at Lloyd's;

- the assets in the Member's Premiums Trust Funds;
- the Central Fund and other net assets of the Society;
- the net wealth of Members.

Liabilities are the aggregate of those reported as at the preceding year end for the most recent closed year of account, the two intervening open years and outstanding years left open.

Liabilities for each syndicate are determined as the greater of the amounts produced by application of formulae agreed with the DTI for different classes of business at Lloyd's, and estimates prepared by the managing agent of that syndicate.

Annual audits of Members' assets and liabilities

The ICA also requires that each Member's assets and liabilities at Lloyd's are audited annually. An audited certificate must be delivered to the DTI which includes a statement as to whether the value of the Member's available assets, which for these purposes includes only its funds at Lloyd's and the assets in its Premiums Trust Funds, are adequate to meet that Member's liabilities in respect of Lloyd's business. Failure to provide the certificate would oblige the underwriter to maintain an individual margin of solvency rather than being able to rely on the global margin maintained by Lloyd's.

Where any Member's assets would otherwise be inadequate for these purposes, the Council has the power to earmark assets in the Central Fund and other assets of the Corporation to make up the shortfall. Any Member so affected is obliged to pay the amount of the shortfall to Lloyd's.

Solvency regulation outside the UK

To satisfy solvency requirements in certain non-UK jurisdictions where Lloyd's is a licensed insurer, Lloyd's annually submits copies of its Global Accounts and the SSOB prepared to ICA requirements to the relevant regulatory authorities of those jurisdictions, in addition to any other specific statistics required by the relevant authority.

Maintaining assets

Many overseas regulators also require Lloyd's to maintain in their jurisdiction assets in the form of cash or liquid investments or to provide letters of credit or guarantees.

More extensive solvency regulation is applied in the US and Canada. Premiums Trust Funds held in local dollars are subject to the relevant trust deeds, irrespective of where the risk originates or where the policy is written. Lloyd's is required to submit filings based on, respectively, Lloyd's US and Canadian dollar assets and liabilities. Lloyd's imposes its own solvency rules on syndicates with the intention of ensuring that the dollar solvency positions are maintained.

EU Directives

The ICA implements certain Directives. These specify Lloyd's as a permitted form of insurance undertaking and contain several adaptations to take account of its particular structure.

Members of Lloyd's do not require independent authorisation from EU member states' regulatory bodies to carry out insurance in the EU through Lloyd's.

WINDING-UP

Members must always meet their liabilities

Leading Counsel has advised that, on a winding-up of the Society, Members would remain liable for their own underwriting obligations, but would have no liability to meet any shortfall in the Society's assets. In principle, therefore, Members' funds at Lloyd's and amounts held under the Premiums Trust Funds in excess of their own several underwriting liabilities would be available to them (subject to the recovery of loans made between Members and syndicates in the course of meeting liabilities for various years of account). However, while the law would take its course, whether in the UK or elsewhere, significant delays in the recovery of assets by solvent Members would arise. Furthermore, it should be assumed that the assets required to be held in deposits in a number of non-UK jurisdictions would not be fully recoverable in these circumstances.

CHAPTER NINE

The framework of security

FINANCIAL CONTROLS

Lloyd's chain of security

INDIVIDUAL MEMBERS	CORPORATE MEMBERS
▼	▼
Premiums Trust Funds No profit can be paid out for 36 months Strict investment criteria	**Premiums Trust Funds** No profit can be paid out for 36 months Strict investment criteria
▼	▼
Funds at Lloyd's 20-50% of overall premium limit held in trust by Lloyd's Strict investment criteria	**Funds at Lloyd's** 50% or more of overall premium limit held in trust by Lloyd's Strict investment criteria Minimum £0.5 million of funds at Lloyd's
▼	
Other personal wealth Resources of members beyond funds at Lloyd's	
▼	▼

New Central Fund
All Members contribute annually, Corporate Members'
contribution rate is two and a half times that of the individual Member.
The Central Fund is available, if other funds are insufficient, to meet all
liabilities arising from policyholders' valid claims, whether the Lloyd's
Member is an individual name or Corporate Member

Lloyd's impeccable claims payment record is in no small part due to its unique four-part system of financial security. Known as the chain of security, the system is designed to protect the interests of Lloyd's policyholders. The following description can be read in conjunction with the diagram at the beginning of this sub-section.

- The First Link
  All premiums accepted by Members of Lloyd's are initially paid into Premiums Trust Funds (every Member is obliged by law to have such a fund). Most policyholders' valid claims will be met from the Funds. Together with the separate US and Canadian dollar Trust Funds, Lloyd's Premium Trust Funds in the aggregate are (31/12/96) valued at just under £7,888 million.

- The Second Link
  In order to begin or continue underwriting, Lloyd's Members must lodge in trust at Lloyd's for the benefit of policyholders a deposit of an amount equal to 20%-50% (depending on liquidity and resources) of the premiums they will write. These "funds at Lloyd's" are available to meet valid claims if a Member's Premiums Trust Funds prove insufficient in the short term. Total "funds at Lloyd's" at 31/12/96 amounted to £5,256 million in aggregate.

- The Third Link
  Members' assets, not held at Lloyd's, and available up to the entire wealth of the Member, or in the case of Corporate Members, the entire assets of the corporate vehicle.

- The Fourth Link
  The New Central Fund of the society is a fund into which all Members make an annual contribution. Its net assets at 31/12/96 was audited at £236 million. The Fund is available at the discretion of the Council of Lloyd's to meet policyholders claims in the event of Members being unable to meet their underwriting liabilities. With effect from 1st January 1997, under the terms of the New Central Fund byelaw, council is empowered to make a call from members' premium trust funds of an amount of up to £200 million.

The aggregate resources of all the Members of Lloyd's, attributable to each of the four links in the chain of security, plus the assets of the Corporation, were at 31.12.96, £14.4 billion.

THE CENTRAL FUND

In principle the Central Fund is applied at the discretion of the Council for the advancement and protection of the Members of the Society in connection with Lloyd's business; in practice, the Fund has been applied primarily as a policyholders' protection fund, to ensure that valid claims are paid even if individual Members are unable to pay their underwriting liabilities.

The policy-holder's protection fund

The Fund also enables the Society to pass the annual solvency test (see below) since it allows for the earmarking of funds in the event of a shortfall at individual Members' level; and can be used to support RITC operation by protecting earlier syndicate Members from the failure of later syndicate Members to meet their reinsurance liabilities.

The Central Fund is critical to Lloyd's competitive position and the attitude adopted towards Lloyd's by regulatory authorities around the world.

In addition, the Central Fund has also been used to support the Lloyd's in-house insurance companies Lioncover and CentreWrite; as stand-by facility to fund deposits for non-UK jurisdictions; and as support for the arrangements made by Lloyd's for Members in financial difficulties.

SOLVENCY TESTING

The Insurance Companies Act (ICA) of 1982 requires that each year Lloyd's deposits a Statutory Statement of Business (SSOB) with the Secretary of State for Trade and Industry in which is included a Statement of Solvency based on the assets and liabilities of all the Members of Lloyd's taken as an aggregated whole, as at the end of the preceding year of account.

Testing continues until a Member's liabilities have all been discharged

It is thereby also a statutory requirement for every Member to comply with a solvency test administered by Lloyd's. The test verifies whether a Member has sufficient acceptable funds to meet their underwriting liabilities and is repeated annually even after a Member has ceased underwriting until all years of account in which they participated have been closed by RITC or by the discharge of all liabilities allocated to that year.

The test is carried out in connection with all the syndicates through which the Member is underwriting. Open year and run-off account surpluses together with the closing year profits on all syndicates in which the Member participates are set off against open year and run-off deficiencies and any closing year losses. Any resulting deficiency is set against the Member's funds at Lloyd's and must, if necessary, be made good by the Member transferring cash or investments from his or her own resources into Premiums Trust Funds.

The ICA also requires each Member's assets and liabilities at Lloyd's to be audited annually, with the delivery to the DTI of an audited certificate.

CHAPTER TEN

The framework of security

RISK EXPOSURE

The nature of the insurance business and Lloyd's structure and accounting cycles mean that a new Member can be potentially exposed to losses from past years of account through long-tail business. This exposure has recently been widened by the exceptional levels of asbestosis-related personal injury and, to a lesser degree, property damage claims from the USA on policies written before 1986. The resulting liabilities have been further swollen by Lloyd's reinsurance of such policies and, more recently, by claims connected with the costs of removing asbestos from buildings. In addition, there have been a number of major, if inconclusive, environmental pollution claims in the USA.

The resolution of these cases and any associated payments to policyholders are likely to be part of a process continuing well into the next century.

The losses and potential losses associated with policies allocated to years of account prior to 1986 are known colloquially as "old years" problems. To help manage them and to limit the exposure to them of Members joining the Society from 1994, Lloyd's has taken a number of special measures.

EQUITAS (FORMERLY NEWCO)

Until the publication of the Lloyd's Reconstruction and Renewal document in May 1995 it was intended to reinsure all liabilities connected with policies originally allocated to the 1985 or prior years of account with Equitas. However, this project was accelerated and expanded to include, in addition, all 1992 and prior year liabilities from both closed and open syndicates. This was done to offer Names 'finality' ie, a final reckoning of all their 1992 and prior year liabilities and with that a chance to resign, subject to regulatory consent. Equitas Reinsurance Limited was given conditional approval by the Department of Trade and Industry in march 1996 and subsequently was given unconditional approval in September 1996.

EXPOSURE TO 1985 AND PRIOR YEARS

A Member's underwriting liabilities at Lloyd's are several. They arise not in respect of Lloyd's or syndicate policies generally but of business which the Member has underwritten. Assuming membership of a syndicate and before the changes instituted by the Council of Lloyd's during 1993 and 1994, there were three principal ways in which a Member could be exposed to claims on policies written into the 1985 and prior years of account:

● The syndicate underwrote risks in the 1985 and prior years of account (or merged with, or succeeded or otherwise reinsured such a syndicate to close) and the liabilities from those years were brought forward to the year in which the Member participated.

● A reinsurance policy allocated to the 1986 or any subsequent year of account and reinsured into the year in which the Member participated provided reinsurance cover (described below) to an insurer or reinsurer in respect of risks incurred in 1985 or prior years.

● Further market levies were required either to cover Central Fund earmarkings relating to 1985 or prior years' underwriting, or to maintain local deposits in certain jurisdictions each of which is available in the last resort to meet liabilities on any Lloyd's policy written there.

Lloyd's measures to counter these exposures are given in the next subsection.

COUNTERING EXPOSURES TO THE PAST

Reinsurance To Close (RITC) into the 1994 and subsequent years of account

No RITC permitted on "old years" A managing agent may not, on behalf of a syndicate Member, accept any RITC of that or any other syndicate if that RITC reinsures any liability for a Lloyd's policy allocated to the 1985 or prior years of account, whether of the syndicate in question or another syndicate. In other words, when effecting RITC into a 1994 or subsequent year of a syndicate, a managing agent may, on behalf of that syndicate, only accept risks attaching to insurance and reinsurance policies allocated to the 1986 and subsequent years of account. Even more specifically, such RITC may not include liabilities under RITC contracts allocated to 1986 and subsequent years written to close the 1985 or any subsequent years of account of that (or any other) syndicate, to the extent that such RITC provides cover for claims arising under or in respect of a policy allocated to the 1985 or prior years of account.

The Council has undertaken that the bye-law incorporating this safeguard will not be amended in a manner which would adversely affect Members underwriting in 1994 without first allowing them an opportunity to give notice of resignation from their syndicates so as to have ceased underwriting from the beginning of the year of account for which the amendment comes into effect. According to leading Counsel, this undertaking gives rise to enforceable rights in favour of the potentially affected underwriting Members.

Post-1985 exposure to "old years" problems

Lloyd's insurance or reinsurance policies and RITC contracts allocated to years of account **later than 1985** may cover liabilities which originally arose in **1985 or before**, or insurable risks referable to that period.

Reinsurance risks from "old years" carried forward

Lloyd's syndicates may, subsequent to 1 January 1986, have reinsured risks written by other insurers (including other Lloyd's syndicates) where the subject of the reinsurance includes risks underwritten in 1985 and prior years.

Such reinsurance policies which include cover in respect of 1985 and prior risks may continue to be underwritten without restriction by Lloyd's syndicates; and liability in respect of those policies may also be carried forward by RITC. In addition, "claims-made" policies allocated to the 1994 and subsequent years of account may, through the time permitted to allow discovery of claims, give rise to a claim which arose through events which took place in 1985 or prior years. The "ring-fence" prohibiting RITC into 1994 and subsequent years of account will not apply to the liabilities underwritten under such policies.

These potential liabilities will all be reinsured into Equitas and be restricted by a proposed extension of the reinsurance to close (restriction) bye-law which prohibits them being carried forward into the future market. As a result prospective Members will only be concerned with liabilities arising out of the 1993 and subsequent years of account through this process of reinsurance to close.

Central Fund contributions and non-UK deposits

The Council has the power to charge subscriptions and to require contributions to be made by Members to the Central Fund. It also has the discretion to apply the Central Fund and all other assets of the Society to meet the liabilities of defaulting Members to the extent that it considers that to do so would advance and protect the interests of the

Protecting Members' interests Members in connection with their Lloyd's business.

The Council has made bye-laws and will undertake to Members to place upper limits on the fees, subscription and Central Fund contributions which may be imposed on underwriting Members in respect of the 1994 and subsequent years of account. These limits may only be exceeded with the approval of a resolution by the majority of underwriting Members who would have to pay the additional contribution.

Contained in the Lloyd's reconstruction and renewal document is a proposal to make a bye-law preventing the proceeds of any such future levy being used in respect of 1992 and prior liabilities.

Non-UK policyholder protection deposits

Local deposits required As a matter of closely related interest, regulatory authorities in a number of non-UK jurisdictions require the maintenance of local deposits for policyholder protection. These deposits (or the costs incurred in procuring them from third parties) may be taken in the form of a loan from the Premiums Trust Funds of Members of syndicates underwriting in those jurisdictions and in the last resort could be applied to meet liabilities on any Lloyd's policies with insurers in the relevant jurisdiction, including policies allocated to the 1985 or prior years of account. Accordingly, Members writing business in these jurisdictions may be indirectly exposed to liabilities relating to 1985 and prior years.

PREMIUMS TRUST FUNDS LOAN LIABILITIES

PTFs - a flexible resource The operation of Premiums Trust Funds takes place on a pooled basis and managing agents have discretionary powers to invest, realise and disburse as they believe to be in the best interests of the syndicates under their management, subject to review by their auditors. Whatever methods are adopted, agents are required to ensure equitable apportionment between the years of account and to make full disclosure in the syndicate annual reports.

A consequence of the managing agents' powers and the varying needs of syndicates and membership is that Premiums Trust Funds can be used as sources of interest - bearing loans to meet a variety of needs, including liabilities in respect of a syndicate's business written in earlier or later years of account or to meet the needs of other Premiums Trust Funds, whether under the original agent's management or those of other agents and to meet a Member's liabilities, in effect making the loan between Members.

Loans between Members might be used to discharge claims in respect of 1985 or prior year policies.

In each case, the managing agent must be satisfied that the loan constitutes a readily realisable asset.

All such loans are recorded as liabilities and assets of the respective Members' Premiums Trust Funds for solvency purposes; a Member's liability to repay any such loan is amongst the liabilities for which cash calls may be made on the Member.

Loans of a similar kind occur in respect of American and Canadian Trust Funds.

PERMANENT RISKS

A high risk business

Insurance underwriting is, by its nature, a high-risk business. Losses may be sustained and, in the worst case, Members' funds eliminated.

IBNR

Each year, outstanding potential liabilities including amounts for claims incurred but not reported ("IBNR") are assessed. In certain circumstances, this may give rise to cash calls on Members before an underwriting year has closed.

Increase of reserves

As part of the annual review of outstanding liabilities, it is possible that provisions previously made for losses subsequently prove inadequate. In such circumstances, the reserves may need strengthening and this obligation would fall to the Members of the year which reinsured those liabilities. By the same token, should reserves subsequently have proved not to be needed, any surplus would be to the benefit of those Members.

Possible cash calls

(See page 33)

MEMBERS' AGENTS' POOLING ARRANGEMENTS (MAPA)

MAPAs -
reducing
individual
risks

MAPA is an arrangement whereby a Members' agent pools underwriting capacity so that the Members are able to participate across a wider spread of syndicates than they usually would through a bespoke underwriting portfolio. This can enable Members to diversify their risk by writing smaller lines across a large range of syndicates. The scheme is similar to the spread of selective risk that characterises unit trusts. In order to participate in MAPA, individual Members have to appoint a Members' agent.

MAPA participants are given safeguards similar to those operating from 1995 for standard syndicate participation:

- Prior approval for terminating a Membership will have to be obtained from the Council by managing agents or Members' agents.

- MAPA Members have the right to withdraw from a MAPA while retaining their underlying syndicate participations above an appropriate minimum level, whether through the same Members' agent or while moving to another Members' agent. This right has to be exercised by 31 October in each year.

- An auction system has now been established which offers MAPA members the opportunity to realise value from their participations by selling the whole or a proportion of their MAPA portfolio.

Pre-emption: It is not practicable for individual members of a MAPA to to be offered pre-emption rights on each underlying syndicate. Instead, a MAPA is treated as a single Member and the MAPA operator decides how much of the MAPA's total entitlement to accept.

LITIGATION

"Old years"
problems

The emergence of the "old years" problems have recently triggered a range of litigation affecting the Society or concerning Members' acceptance into membership and/or the conduct of their underwriting business at Lloyd's.

Litigation affecting the Society most commonly concerns either Members suing Lloyd's or Lloyd's seeking repayment from Members of monies paid from or earmarked against the Central Fund in respect of their underwriting liabilities. A number of actions have also been initiated against agents by Members, often in action groups, seeking compensation on a number of different grounds, including allegedly negligent underwriting on their behalf, under-reserving and misrepresentation.

Actions against the Society

Actions have been initiated by groups of Members against the Society both in the UK and outside. In general, the groups outside the UK are seeking to avoid their underwriting obligations on the grounds of negligent or fraudulent misrepresentations alleged to have been made by the Society through its agents or, in some cases, on the basis of alleged breach of local securities laws.

Jurisdiction remains with the English courts

The Society has argued that these actions should not be heard on various grounds, including the provisions in the Lloyd's general undertaking that commits Members to submit to the jurisdiction of the English courts and that provide that any dispute is to be governed by English law. This argument has in principle been accepted by the courts in Australia, Canada, New Zealand and the USA.

In the UK, the actions include the seeking of an injunction to prevent the application of Members' deposits to meet underwriting liabilities; and the argument that the Society owed a duty of care to Members and had negligently breached that duty. A preliminary injunction has been refused by the judiciary; and the duty of care has been held to have been non-existent.

Two complaints have been made to the EU Commission in which Members allege breaches by the Society of Articles 85 and 86 of the Treaty of Rome. Consideration of these complaints remains at an early stage and they are being vigorously opposed by Lloyd's.

Actions by the Society

Current actions by Lloyd's are mainly for the recovery of monies paid from the Central Fund to prevent Members defaulting on their underwriting commitments.

Recovering funds

Lloyd's is now pursuing such actions where necessary for the recovery of amounts drawn down from the Central Fund.

Lloyd's has obtained judgment against a number of Canadian banks which had been refusing to honour draw-downs under certain letters of credit issued to Lloyd's by the banks on behalf of a number of Canadian Members.

Actions against Members' agents

"Pay now, sue later" Numerous actions were brought by Members against agents, and prior to the 'settlement' of litigation in 1996 some had achieved notable success. Where Lloyd's commences actions against Members for recovery of monies applied from, or earmarked against, the Central Fund, the Members concerned may make counter-claims, raising some of the issues in the actions against agents.

The Court of Appeal has upheld the judgment that the "pay now sue later" clause in the standard managing agents' agreement only precludes a Member from making legal challenge to, for example, the agent's estimate of liabilities until the Member has paid a cash call; but, by contrast, did not preclude a Member from pursuing allegations that the claim arose from negligent underwriting without first satisfying the call.

Legal dispute settlement initiative

As a result of the publication of the Reconstruction and Renewal document a new settlement initiative was undertaken with the aim of securing a comprehensive negotiated settlement of the intra-market litigation. Lloyd's continued to try to build a consensus in its dialogue with the litigating parties as to the constitution of an acceptable settlement. This initiative was brought to a successful conclusion in September 1996 when the great majority of parties concerned reached agreement.

Lioncover Insurance Company Ltd

Wholly-owned specialist reinsurance vehicle Lioncover is a wholly-owned Lloyd's subsidiary which was formed as a vehicle to reinsure the liabilities of 73 syndicates managed by former agencies. They wrote broad-based marine, non-marine and aviation accounts, which included a large exposure to non-marine long-tail casualty business. The Society is liable to fund the amount by which the company's liabilities exceed its assets. Such funding will come from the

Central Fund or other assets of the Society.

Up to the end of December 1996 a total of £487 million has been paid from the Central Fund to Lioncover. During 1996 agreement was reached with certain Reinsurers on substantial Reinsurance programmes which had been disputed. It is envisaged that all liabilities of Lioncover will ultimately be Reinsured into Equitas once terms have been agreed. Almost all Lioncover's business relates to 1985 and prior years of account and will therefore fall within the scope of Equitas.

CentreWrite Limited

Another wholly-owned subsidiary of the Society, CentreWrite was formed to provide reinsurance on an arm's-length, commercial basis for syndicates in run-off and for individual Members of such syndicates. Any inadequacies in the funds of CentreWrite will be met from the Central Fund or other assets of the society. In its accounts for 1996 CentreWrite declared a pretax profit of £47.5 million. As a result the board of Centre-Write has agreed to pay to the Central Fund £33.8 million, representing a refund of calls previously made upon the Fund.

Wholly-owned reinsurance vehicle for syndicates in run-off

Appendixes

A summary of rules governing Corporate Membership

1.1 REQUIREMENTS

The use of the word 'Member' in this section refers to Corporate Member.

The requirements arise principally under the bye-laws of the Society and the conditions and requirements to be made under them, and any agreements and instruments made pursuant to any of those conditions or requirements. The following constitute a summary only.

1.1.1 Structural

● Members must be companies which have not traded, incorporated with limited or unlimited liability within the European Union or any other jurisdictions.

● Share capital of Members must be in registered form: bearer shares will not be acceptable.

● Subject to sections 1.1.4 and 1.1.5, below, Lloyd's will impose no restrictions on the free transferability of shares in a Corporate Member. Restrictions may, however, be imposed under applicable external legal or regulatory requirements.

NOTE: Although the Council requires copies of a Member's memorandum and articles of association (or equivalent constitutional documents) to be submitted with its application for membership (and any amendments to be submitted thereafter), these documents will not be vetted or approved by the Council.

1.1.2 Funds at Lloyd's

● Every Corporate Member must provide and maintain funds at Lloyd's valued at not less than the highest of:

    • 50% or such greater percentage of its overall premium limit (OPL) for the next following year of account as may be determined by Lloyd's for that Corporate Member

~REQUIREMENTS~

- The amount which was required to be provided in any previous year of account which has not been closed by reinsurance to close

- £0.5 million

In the case of successor Corporate Members incorporated outside the United States of America the concessionary minimum will apply. In the case of a Corporate Member incorporated in any state of the United States of America the amount required will be £1.5 million.

- The minimum Lloyd's deposit for Corporate Members will be £500,000 (which will support an OPL of £1 million). The Council's current proposals regarding the assets which must comprise this deposit are summarised in Appendix III.

- A Corporate Member is required to maintain minimum funds at Lloyd's equal to 50% of its OPL. A Corporate Member's funds at Lloyd's will initially comprise a capital deposit (known as a 'Lloyd's Deposit') which is held by Lloyd's on specified trusts. This may be provided by the Member itself, or, with the consent of the Council, by a third party for the Corporate Member's benefit. The Council will review this percentage in subsequent years of account having regard to the need to ensure security for policy-holders and the introduction of risk-based weightings reflecting the different lines of business underwritten by individual syndicates.

- A summary of the Council's current proposals regarding the provision of bank guaran-tees and letters of credit as permitted investments is also set out in Appendix III. The benefit of bank guarantees and letters of credit will be held by Lloyd's as trustee under a Security and Trust Deed. Shares or other securities in Corporate Members will not be acceptable as part of a Member's funds at Lloyd's.

- The assets comprising a Corporate Member's Lloyd's deposit must be kept free and clear of all liens, charges and encumbrances and may only be released in accordance with the terms of the Deposit Trust Deeds.

- Subject to the procedures laid down in the Deposit Trust Deeds, interest and dividends on the assets comprising a Corporate Member's deposit may be distributed to the Corporate Member or to a nominated person authorised under the Financial Services Act 1986 to manage the assets comprised in its funds at Lloyd's within the permitted investment criteria and subject to detailed safeguards.

1.1.3 Restriction of activities

- A Member's activities must be exclusively dedicated to underwriting insurance business at Lloyd's for its own account and directly ancillary activities. For example, the Member may take out stop-loss reinsurance and (subject to the relevant trust deeds) nominate a person authorised under the Financial Services Act 1986 to manage the investments comprising its funds at Lloyd's and cash resources and (subject to Council approval) hedge its foreign exchange exposures. The Member will not be permitted to undertake any other insurance or reinsurance business.

- Investments by the Member will not be permitted in other Members or in a company in the same group as a Member. No single holding shall exceed 15% of the overall value of a Member's funds, except those listed in para 1 of Appendix III 'Narrower Range Assets'.

1.1.4 Control of Members

Without the prior written consent of the Council, no person may be a "controller" of a Member. For this purpose a "controller" is any person:

- who either alone or with any connected person is entitled to exercise, or control the exercise of, 10% or more of the voting power at any general meeting of the Member or of another body corporate by which it is controlled; or

- in accordance with whose directions or instructions (either alone or with those of any connected person) the directors or the Member are accustomed to act.

Control is therefore construed accordingly.

- A "connected person" in relation to any person means:

  - any person who is party to any agreement, arrangement or understanding with the first person involving mutual obligations, understandings or expectations with regard to the retention or disposal of any shares in a body corporate or to the exercise of any voting power conferred by such shares or to any other influence arising from such shares;

  - any person whom the first person controls;

  - where that person is a body corporate, any trustee of its pensions funds;

- where that person is a body corporate, its directors and their associates;
- where that person is an individual, his or her associates.

● "Associates" are:
  - a person's spouse and children (including step-children and adopted children) under the age of 18 years;
  - any body corporate of which that person or their spouse is a director;
  - any person who is an employer, employee or partner of the person or of their spouse; and
  - any body corporate of which the person or their spouse, either alone or with any other connected person, has control.

● The Council will not normally grant consent to a person to be a controller of more than one Member unless the OPL of each Member controlled by that person exceeds £20 million or, in the case of a Member which is a wholly-owned subsidiary of a body corporate whose equity shares are listed on a recognised stock exchange, when the Council may exercise its discretion to grant consent if each controlled Member has an OPL of not less than £10 million. However, the Council is unlikely to agree to more than ten Members being controlled by the same person unless the controller is a substantial publicly-listed company.

● If consent is granted for the purposes stated in the preceding paragraph, the Council reserves the right to require appropriate undertakings. These are likely to include an undertaking from each of the controlled Members (supported by a commitment from the controller) that if one of them fails to meet any of its Lloyd's obligations:
  - Lloyd's will be entitled to require the others to cease or reduce their underwriting and/or
  - having regard to the fact that the Central Fund may be applied to discharge the obligations of the defaulting Member, Lloyd's will be entitled to require each of the other controlled Members, not withstanding the limits referred to in section 1.1.10, to make contributions to the Central Fund up to the amount of their respective net profits held from time to time in Premiums Trust Funds, sufficient to reimburse the Central Fund in full for any payment made on behalf of the defaulting Member.

● A Member may not sell, transfer or assign the benefit of its syndicate participations.

1.1.5 "Fit and proper" requirement

- The Council has absolute discretion to determine whether an existing or prospective Member is "fit and proper". In arriving at its determination, the Council will have regard to any facts or circumstances it considers appropriate. For example, the Council reserves the right to decline an application if it considers that the Member would, while otherwise meeting the requirements of Corporate Membership, in the view of the Council be likely to jeopardise the standing of Lloyd's with its policyholders or its regulators.

- Without limiting its discretion, the Council may have regard to the character and composition of the board of directors and management of the Member and to the reputation and financial standing of the Member's "controllers", bodies corporate under common control with a Member and "major shareholders". A person will be considered to be a "major shareholder" of a Member where they have the right, either alone or with any connected person, to exercise, or to control the exercise of, 15% or more of the voting power at any general meeting of the Member or of another body corporate by which it is controlled.

- There is no restriction on Members' agents, managing agents, brokers or Lloyd's advisers having interests in securities of Members or a person who controls a Member. However, all such interests will require immediate disclosure to the Council and a register of the interests disclosed will be open for inspection.

- The form of application for Members of the Society will require details of the Member's directors, managers, controllers, major shareholders and companies under common control with it. Under the Membership Bye-law the Member will be obliged to notify Lloyd's of material changes to this information.

- Under the Membership Bye-law, no person may become a controller, director, major shareholder or manager of a Member without the prior written consent of Lloyd's.

- The applicant's sponsor is required to review the corporate applicant's application and supporting documentation and information in order to satisfy itself that the application has been properly prepared after due and careful enquiry.

- The Council may at any time (and without any liability in consequence thereof) determine that a Member is not fit and proper, whereupon such Member will be required to cease underwriting. Provisions regarding a Member's right of appeal are set out in the Appeal Tribunal and Membership Bye-laws.

1.1.6 Lloyd's advisers

- Each Corporate Member must retain one or more Lloyd's advisers to provide syndicate analysis services and to negotiate syndicate participation on its behalf. Corporate Members which prefer to appoint a Members' agent to manage all or part of their Lloyd's affairs are free to do so.

- Under the Membership Bye-law the Council has power to dispense with the requirement that a Corporate Member appoints and retains a Lloyd's adviser. The council would normally expect to exercise this power in relation to a Corporate Member which has appropriate syndicate analysis skills itself or is to be advised in relation to Lloyd's by a Member of its group possessing those skills. A Corporate Member may not, however, become a Lloyd's adviser itself, nor may it advise other Members in its group.

- A Corporate Member will be free to negotiate its terms of engagement and its fees with its Lloyd's adviser(s) but the terms must be set out in writing. Lloyd's also has power to prescribe terms for inclusion in those terms of engagement.

- All Members' agents registered as such on 8 September 1993 automatically qualify as Lloyd's advisers. In approving a Lloyd's adviser (or Members' agent), Lloyd's does not accept any liability to the relevant Corporate Member or to any holders of shares or other securities in the Member. It will be the responsibility of each Corporate Member to satisfy itself as to the skill, competence and financial standing of its chosen Lloyd's adviser(s) or Members' agent(s).

- There will be no prohibition on a suitably qualified Lloyd's adviser also acting as a sponsor.

- A Corporate Member must, prior to 31 October in each year, arrange for its Lloyd's adviser(s) or Members' agent(s) to prepare, or must itself prepare, an analysis and commentary on the syndicates which it is proposing to join for the succeeding year and deliver this to Lloyd's.

1.1.7 Promotion of corporate applicants

- The marketing, distribution and trading of the share capital in corporate applicants and Members will be a matter for their promoters, directors and advisers and the relevant securities laws and regulations of all applicable jurisdictions. Lloyd's accepts no responsibility or liability in this regard.

- All prospectuses, filings and marketing documents issued by or on behalf of the

Corporate Member prior to its admission to membership and all amendments or supplements must be sent to Lloyd's at or before the time of issue. However, Lloyd's will not undertake any verification or vetting of any such documents and accepts no responsibility or liability in this regard.

- The sponsor's declaration referred to in section 1.1.8 below and the legal opinion referred to in section 1.1.9 below are required in order to satisfy Lloyd's that all applicable legal and regulatory requirements relating to the formation and promotion of the corporate applicant have been complied with.

1.1.8 The sponsor

- Each application for Corporate Membership must be supported by a sponsor, who must be suitably qualified (professionally and financially) to provide the declaration referred to below. In most instances, the sponsor will be an independent merchant or investment bank, stockbroker or accountant experienced in the formation of companies and the distribution and marketing of shares and securities. In approving the sponsor, Lloyd's will have regard to all relevant circumstances, including the size of the applicant for Corporate Membership, the number and type of shareholders (eg, whether they are individuals or institutions), the place of incorporation, the jurisdictions in which the corporate applicant's shares are distributed or marketed, the sponsor's reputation and standing and its experience and understanding of Lloyd's. Lloyd's will have an absolute discretion as to whether or not to approve a sponsor. In approving a sponsor Lloyd's accepts no responsibility or liability to a Corporate Member or any holders of its shares or other securities.

- The sponsor will be responsible, *inter alia*, for:

  - ensuring that the Corporate Applicant has been properly advised as regards its formation and the distribution and marketing of its shares;

  - reviewing the corporate applicant's and supporting documentation and information and satisfying itself that the application has been properly prepared after due and careful enquiry;

  - ensuring that the corporate applicant and its directors are aware of their obligations under the membership agreement and the other agreements and instruments to which it is required to become a party prior to or on admission to membership;

  - and ensuring that all material facts are brought to the attention of the Council which might be relevant to its assessment of the application.

- The sponsor will be required to provide Lloyd's with a declaration (which will be private and confidential to Lloyd's) covering the matters referred to in section 1.1.8 and any other matter relating to the application which Lloyd's may require.

- Lloyd's reserves the right to require at any time either a general or specific confirmation from the sponsor as a condition of allowing a Corporate Member to continue to underwrite. An example of when Lloyd's would be likely to require such a confirmation is when the Corporate Member is proposing to increase its OPL by a significant amount and to finance such increase by a further issue of shares.

1.1.9 Membership agreement and legal opinion

- Each Corporate Member will be required to enter into membership agreement with Lloyd's in a prescribed form which will incorporate the requirements and undertakings of Corporate Membership and contain a number of formal assurances in favour of Lloyd's.

- Before admission to membership a corporate applicant will be required to provide Lloyd's with a legal opinion of a lawyer approved for this purpose by Lloyd's which opinion may, in relation to questions of law in jurisdictions where the lawyer concerned is not qualified to advise, be supported by legal opinions of lawyers who are so qualified, confirming, *inter alia*, that:

  - the corporate applicant has been duly incorporated and has the corporate capacity to become an underwriting Member of Lloyd's and to enter into and perform insurance contracts written on its behalf as a syndicate Member and certain other specified agreements and instruments;

  - the trust deeds constituting the Premiums Trust Funds and the corporate applicant's funds at Lloyd's will be recognised as valid dispositions effective in accordance with their terms and there is no rule of law of the jurisdiction in which the corporate applicant is incorporated which would entitle the corporate applicant or any liquidator or creditor to assert any interest in or other right to the assets held under those deeds otherwise than in accordance with the relevant trust deed; and

  - the choice of English law in the various agreements and instruments and the submission of the Corporate Member to the jurisdiction of the English Courts will be fully recognised in its country of incorporation and that all judgments against the Corporate Member will be enforceable in that country.

- The legal opinion provided under section 1.1.9 above must be renewed or confirmed as part of the declaration of compliance to be given by a member as at 30 November each year as a condition of continued underwriting.

1.1.10 Subscriptions, fees and contributions

- In addition to managing agents' and Lloyd's advisers' fees and commissions, a Corporate Member presently is required to pay to Lloyd's the following fees and contributions (plus VAT, where applicable):

  - **application fee:** this is a non-refundable fixed fee of £10,000 (plus VAT) payable on application which will be applied by Lloyd's in defraying the cost of processing the application for membership.

  - **Members' subscriptions:** these finance the Corporation's central costs (apart from those allocated to syndicates or to Members individually for particular services provided to them which will continue to be charged without any maximum limits) and will not exceed 0.5% of allocated capacity for 1997 for all members; and

  - **Central Fund contribution:** the annual Central Fund contribution for Corporate Members has been set at 1.5% of allocated capacity for the 1997 year of account.

- Except with the approval of Members as referred to in section 1.1.11 below, the 1994 Annual Subscription and the Central Fund contribution referred to above will not be increased. In each of the 1995, 1996 and 1997 years of account the Annual Contribution will not exceed 1.5% of allocated capacity for Corporate Members (and 0.6% for individual Members). It should be clearly understood that in relation to 1995, 1996 and 1997 these limits should not be construed as an indication as to what the level of the Annual Subscription and Central Fund contributions will actually be.

- For the 1995 and subsequent years of account, prior notice of the annual subscriptions and Central Fund contributions will be given prior to 30th September in the year prior to commencement of the year of account in which the amendment is to take effect. Accordingly, underwriting members will know the subscriptions and contributions payable prior to the commencement of the new year, and no additional or special levies can be imposed on the underwriting members of the year in question in respect of that or any other year of account without the approval of the Members as referred to in section 1.1.11 below.

● As regards losses and liabilities arising in respect of 1993 and prior years, the Council reserves the right to levy additional Central Fund contributions on those who are Members of the 1993 and prior years of account.

● At any time after the commencement of a year of account, a special contribution recommended by the Council as being reasonable and in the interests of the Society as a whole may be imposed on the Members underwriting in that year of account over and above the limits referred to in section 1.1.11 below with the approval of a resolution of the Members affected. Members entitled to vote on any proposed special contribution will be limited to corporate and individual Members underwriting in the year in question and voting rights will be proportionate to Members' liability to contribute.

● Appropriate changes have been made to the bye-laws in order to introduce these safeguards and the Council has undertaken to the Members underwriting in the 1994 and subsequent years of account that these safeguards will not be amended in a manner which would have an adverse effect on such Members unless the Members in question are given the opportunity to resign from their syndicates so as to cease to be underwriting Members with effect from the beginning of the year of account in which the amendment comes into effect. For this purpose, at least three months' notice of the proposed amendment will be given prior to the commencement of the year of account in which the amendment is to become effective and, in any event, no amendment may be made to take effect earlier than the beginning of the 1998 year of account.

● The provisions of section 1.1.11 will not apply to any additional Central Fund contributions payable pursuant to any capacity management procedures introduced by the Council described in section 1.1.4 or to the Central Fund contribution payable in relation to qualifying quota share arrangements or to the Central Fund contributions payable in the circumstances.

1.1.11 Spread of syndicate participation

● For the 1995 year of account, a Corporate Member was, except as permitted in section 1.1.12 below, required to diversify its underwriting so that not more than 20% of its OPL was allocated to any one syndicate. This restriction has now been removed but Council retains the right to amend the corporate solvency ratios.

● If any Corporate Member or group of Corporate Members under the same control accounts for more than 5% of a syndicate's allocated capacity, this will be required to be disclosed to the Council.

- In the event of a breach of the limits described above and following a disclosure under the preceeding paragraph, the Council will have the power to require the Corporate Member concerned to cease underwriting, to reduce its underwriting participations or to provide additional funds at Lloyd's. The Council will also have the power if, in its sole and absolute discretion, it determines that the amount and spread of a Corporate Member's participations would otherwise represent an unacceptable risk to the Central Fund or the Society's other resources.

- It must be emphasised that Lloyd's can accept no responsibility for the application of these diversity rules or for agreeing to any variation. In every case, it will be for the Corporate Member to satisfy itself as to the allocation of its OPL and the spread of risk involved.

- The introduction of risk weighting in future years is likely to result in a variation in the required level of funds at Lloyd's reflecting the risk of different classes of business.

1.1.12 Accounting

- Each Corporate Member will be responsible for preparing its own statutory accounts in accordance with the statutory and other requirements applicable to it.

- Lloyd's will not impose any requirements regarding the accounting reference date of Corporate Members. Nevertheless, it will be a requirement that each Corporate Member should deliver to Lloyd's copies of its financial statements not later than six months after its financial year end. These financial statements must be audited by a firm of accountants of good standing to be approved by Lloyd's. The Membership Bye-law provides that accounts must be drawn up to, and audited in accordance with, the standards applied by the Companies Act 1985 or, in the case of a member incorporated in the European Community but not in the UK, the harmonised standards applied across the Community by the Fourth Council Directive.

1.1.13 Winding-up

- Without the consent of the Council, a Corporate Member may not pass a resolution providing for its winding-up or liquidation and may not cause or allow to occur certain other specified insolvency events.

1.1.14 Approved jurisdictions

● A Corporate Member may be created, formed or incorporated in any one of the following jurisdictions:

- any member state for the time being of the European Union (EU);
- any state of Australia;
- Bermuda;
- British Virgin Islands;
- Guernsey;
- Hong Kong;
- Iceland;
- Isle of Man;
- Japan;
- Jersey;
- Mauritius;
- Netherlands, Antilles;
- New Zealand;
- Norway;
- Republic of South Africa;
- Singapore;
- Switzerland, and
- any state of the United States of America.

● The Council will consider extending qualifying jurisdictions of incorporation where it is satisfied in relation to the legal and regulatory consequences. Equally, it may determine that a jurisdiction (other than an EU Member State jurisdiction) should cease to be as qualifying jurisdiction for legal or regulatory reasons. In such circumstances the Council would give the maximum notice practicable to enable Corporate Members incorporated in that jurisdiction to rearrange their affairs.

ADMISSION OF NON-EU MEMBERS

1.2.1 United States jurisdiction

In many states in the US, the admission of Members to Lloyd's requires regulatory approval and/or statutory amendment in order for Lloyd's trading privileges to continue. Necessary approvals and/or amendments have been secured in several states and are being pursued in others with particular emphasis on those most commercially significant for Lloyd's.

Members' agents annually file "Form Ds" with the United States Securities and Exchange Commission (the SEC) in respect of each new individual US Member and should continue to do so. To the extent that they raise capital in the US, Members will have to comply with US Securities laws and regulations.

1.2.2 Other jurisdictions

Legislative amendments to take account of the admission of Members will also be required in certain other jurisdictions. In most cases, non-UK legal advice has been that existing (local) legislation requires no amendment. Nonetheless, the insurance regulatory authorities in all relevant jurisdictions are being notified of the decision to admit Members. None has to date indicated that this will affect Lloyd's continuing ability to conduct insurance business as before.

Applicants for membership must satisfy themselves as to compliance with any non-UK securities or insurance law or regulation which may apply to their insurance or fund-raising activities.

1.3 TAXATION

1.3.1 General

A Corporate Member will be subject to UK corporation tax on the profits arising to it by virtue of its underwriting activities. In addition and in common with individual Members, Corporate Members may be subject to tax in the US and Canada on their

Lloyd's income and gains attributable to a permanent establishment in the US and Canada.

1.3.2 U.K. tax arrangements for Corporate Members

The Inland Revenue issued a statement covering the proposed tax arrangements for Corporate Members on 14 October 1993. Sections 219 to 230 and 248 of the Finance Act 1994 incorporated these proposals and is the legislation dealing with the UK tax regime. It applies from 1 January 1994.

The legislation provides that:

- except for the special rules set out below, a Corporate Member of Lloyd's will be chargeable to corporation tax and subject to the corporation tax pay and file rules in the normal way.

- a Corporate Member's profits from membership of Lloyd's syndicates or assets in the funds in which its premiums received are invested ("premiums trust funds") will be charged to tax as income under the rules applying to Schedule D Case I. In addition, profits arising to a Corporate Member from funds other than premiums trust funds (referred to as "ancillary trust funds") or from the other assets used in its underwriting business will be charged to tax as income under Schedule D Case I if they would not otherwise be charged to tax as income;

- profits and losses from syndicate participations and assets forming part of a premiums trust fund are treated as accruing evenly over the underwriting year in which (in the case of syndicate participation profits) they are declared or (in the case of profits or losses from premiums trust fund assets) to which they are allocated under the rules of practices of Lloyd's;

- income and gains other than those which arise from membership of a syndicate or from premiums trust fund assets will be taxable as income in the same way as for corporate insurers generally; and

- there will be special rules specifically for items such as stop-loss insurance, premiums trust fund assets, reinsurance to close and cessation.

- there is no provision for a special reserve fund for Corporate Members equivalent to that provided for individual members. Nor is it covered by the new equalisation reserves for corporate insurers. Lloyd's have made representations to and are in discussion with the Inland Revenue on the need for a form of reserve fund for corporate members.

1.3.3 US tax

- All Corporate Members, regardless of where they are organised, will be considered to be engaged in a trade or business through a permanent establishment in the US, and will be subject to US tax on income from their US connected business.

- US connected business will generally consist of underwriting profits (and losses) arising from direct insurance and reinsurance premiums placed through a US broker, as well as that portion of the LATF investment income attributable to such premiums.

- Corporate Members will generally compute their taxable profit or loss with respect to US business in a manner similar to US insurances companies, including the discounting of reserves (subject to some special rules).

- Corporate Members will be subject to US tax at the 35% or lower treaty rates on US source investment income which is not attributable to US connected business. For UK Corporate Members, the treaty reduces the rate to 15% in the case of US source dividends and eliminates the tax with respect to interest.

- It is expected that the annual US reporting and filing requirements with respect to the Lloyd's income of any non-US Corporate Members will be included in the Lloyd's First Level Tax Return which is prepared by LeBoeuf, Lamb, Greene & MacRae, Lloyd's US General Counsel. It is also anticipated that any US tax liability will initially be funded by the syndicates, which will be reimbursed from the Corporate Member's distribution.

1.3.4 Canadian Tax

Corporate and individual Members of Lloyd's are treated as having a place of business in Canada. They are taxed on any Canadian Business coming into Lloyd's via binding authorities, together with an appropriate proportion of the Lloyd's Canadian Trust Fund.

1.3.5 UK Value Added Tax

Corporate Members are able to register for VAT. They will have a fixed recovery rate in respect of their underwriting activities based on the rate currently available to all existing Members' agents and notified to the Market on a quarterly basis by the Lloyd's Taxation Department. (the Global Market Recovery Rate).

1.3.6 Resignation

Members may terminate their agency agreements with their Members' agents or managing agents by giving written notice of their intention by 31 August in any year, to be effective in respect of syndicate participations at the end of that year.

Members may start the process of resigning from Lloyd's by giving written notice to Lloyd's. Received before 31 August, the Member's underwriting will cease at the end of that year; received after that date, the Members may have to continue underwriting for the following year if the Members' agents are not able to terminate all their syndicate participations by the end of that year.

Upon ceasing to underwrite, Members remain non-underwriting Members until their Lloyd's involvements have been wound up, ie, until the last year of account is closed or their liabilities are reinsured and all underwriting losses have been discharged; this may take a number of years. Until this occurs, the funds which Members have lodged at Lloyd's are retained by the trustees. The Council of Lloyd's has the power to shorten or extend the period during which a Member must remain a non-underwriting Member.

Conversion to Corporate Membership

A short summary of the rules Governing Conversion from Unlimited Trading to Limited Liability Trading.

Introduction

From the beginning of the 1995 year of account, Members trading individually as sole traders with unlimited liability (names) can choose to convert their underwriting arrangements into corporate form. Rules have been introduced which permit the trading of corporate vehicles known as Successor Corporate Members with a lower minimum funds at Lloyd's requirements than the Corporate Members detailed in the previous appendix.

Requirements

Conversion of underwriting to corporate form falls into two main categories: transition and interavailability. A transitional arrangement involves the name transferring the whole of his continuing underwriting business at Lloyd's (by the reinsurance of all open and run-off years of account) to a Successor Corporate Member. An interavailability arrangement is where the name makes his funds at Lloyd's available to support both his past underwriting and the future underwriting of that name's Successor Corporate Member by the variation of certain trust deeds.

Transitional Arrangements

In all respects the Successor Corporate Members (being those resulting from conversion and wholly owned beneficially by the natural name or names who underwent conversion to create them) will need to comply with the requirements outlined in the previous appendix, subject to the following concessions:

● A reduction in the minimum funds at Lloyd's requirements from £500,000 to

£100,000.

- If two or more natural names enter into a conversion arrangement setting up a single successor Corporate Member the minimum funds at Lloyd's requirement will be £100,000 per shareholder/transferor name and not £100,000 in total.

- Approval of a standard Transfer Agreement for Transition to enable the transfer of a natural name's underwriting to their successor Corporate Member.

- A reduction of the initial Corporate Membership fee from £10,000 per Corporate Member to a fee to be fixed by Lloyd's in each case which can be waived in certain circumstances (pertaining to use of Lloyd's standard Transfer Agreements).

- Relaxation of some of the restrictions on composition of funds at Lloyd's for successor Corporate Members for a concessionary period up to the end of the 1999 year of account, such concessions to have expired prior to "coming into line" for the 2000 year of account. This will include the use of Guarantees or Letter of Credit supported by a principal private residence.

- Such successor Corporate Members with funds at Lloyd's of less than £500,000 (small successor Corporate Members) which are party to conversion arrangements are given permission to underwrite for a period of five years only after their commencement. Only in exceptional circumstances will this period be extended.

Interavailability

The rules established for interavailability contain many of the same requirements as for transition. However, there are some important differences. These are:

- Interavailability involves making funds at Lloyd's available to support both past underwriting of a Member and future underwriting of a successor Corporate Member. It does not involve the transfer of a natural name's continuing underwriting business to their successor Corporate Member.

- In order to facilitate the supporting of both past and future underwriting certain amendments are required to the deposit trust deed and/or security and trust deed.

In all respects for a natural name to be eligible for conversion to Corporate Membership under the interavailability rules he must have met all the same financial requirements as he would were he planning to underwrite as a natural name for the subsequent year.

Interavailability provides more flexibility and allows a name the option of ceasing to trade altogether on an unlimited basis or possibly continuing to trade on a reduced level as an individual and trade with limited liability through a successor Corporate Member with the interavailable funds.

Taxation

There are certain tax implications relating to both transition and interavailability which are important. The proposals referred to as transition have been developed with two particular tax effects in mind which would not be available for names converting through interavailability or for resigned names.

- It is intended that any liability of natural names to capital gains tax on the transfer of funds at Lloyd's to the successor Corporate Member be relieved by means of the roll-over relief on incorporation of a trade in Section 162 TCGA/1992.

- It is intended that the relief under section 386 ICTA/1988 should be available to enable the natural name to set tax losses from their prior personal underwriting against income they receive from the successor Corporate Member.

- The obtaining of the above reliefs will obviously be subject to the applicable conditions being met to the satisfaction of the inland revenue.

Scottish Limited Partnerships

A partnership as constitued under the laws of Scotland and in accordance with partnership Act 1980 and the 1907 Act.

In addition to Limited Liability companies, Scottish Limited Partnerships have been approved by Lloyd's for membership purposes with effect from the beginning of 1997.

They are of interest since they provide the protection of a limited liability structure whilst at the same time offer a tax transparency, enabling profit and losses to be assessed/relieved as part of each partners general income.

APPENDIX III

Investment criteria for Funds at Lloyd's

1. Narrower-range assets

The following investments shall constitute narrower-range assets:

i   Fixed-interest securities issued by Her Majesty's Government in the United Kingdom and registered in the United Kingdom, the Government of Northern Ireland or the Government of the Isle of Man, provided that Defence Bonds, national Savings Certificates, Ulster Savings Certificates, Ulster Development Bonds, National Development Bonds, British Savings Bonds, National Savings Income Bonds, National Savings Deposit Bonds, National Savings Indexed-Income Bonds and Deposits in the National Savings Bank or in a bank or department thereof certified under sub-section 3 of section 9 of the Finance Act 1956, are excluded from this sub-paragraph;

ii   Treasury bills;

iii   Tax Reserve Certificates;

iv   Variable interest securities issued by Her Majesty's Government in the United Kingdom and registered in the United Kingdom

v   Securities the payment of interest on which is guaranteed by her Majesty's Government in the United Kingdom or the Government of Northern Ireland;

vi   Fixed-interest securities issued in the United Kingdom by any public authority or nationalised industry or undertaking in the United Kingdom;

vii   Fixed-interest securities issued in the United Kingdom by the government of any overseas territory within the Commonwealth or by any public or local authority within such a territory, being securities registered in the United Kingdom;

viii Securities issued in the United Kingdom by the government of an overseas territory within the Commonwealth or by any public or local authority within such a territory, being securities registered in the United Kingdom and in respect of which the rate of interest is variable by reference to one or more of the following:

    a) the Bank of England's minimum lending rate;

    b) the average rate of discount on allotment on 91-day treasury bills;

c) a yield on 91-day treasury bills;

d) a London sterling inter-bank offered rate;

e) a London sterling certificate of deposit rate.

ix Fixed-interest securities issued in the United Kingdom by the African Development Bank, the Asian Development Bank, the Caribbean Development Bank, the International Finance Corporation, the International Monetary Fund, the International Bank for Reconstruction and Development, the Inter-American Development Bank, the European Atomic Energy Community, the European Community/Union, the European Investment Bank or the European Coal and Steel Community;

References in this sub-paragraph to an overseas territory or to the government of such territory shall be construed as if they occurred in the Overseas Service Act 1958;

a) Subject to paragraph 2.2, US Government securities;

b) Subject to paragraph 2.2, Canadian Government securities;

c) deposits in pounds sterling or an approved foreign currency, provided that all deposits are held in the United Kingdom in an interest-bearing account opened with an approved credit institution;

d) certificates of deposit issued by an approved credit institution with a duration from the date of issue of not more than six months, provided that all certificates of deposit are held in the United Kingdom; and

e) units in UK-authorised unit trusts investing wholly in UK Government securities.

2. Wider-range assets

1A. The following investments shall constitute wider-range assets:

i   Securities, other than those listed in sub-paragraph (g) below, issued or guaranteed by a company incorporated in England, Wales or Scotland which:

ii are of a class quoted or listed on the London Stock Exchange or held in Euroclear or CEDEL S.A.;

iii are issued by a company with a market capitalisation of at least £200 million or a subsidiary of such a company; and

iv are of a class of security having an aggregate market value of at least £100 million.

B. Subject to paragraph 2.2, Securities issued or guaranteed by a company incorporated in any state of the United States of America or Mexico which:

i   are of a class quoted or listed on the New York Stock Exchange, the American stock Exchange or NASDQ;

ii are issued by a company with an equity market capitalisation of at least US$500 million or a subsidiary of such a company;

iii are of a class of security having an aggregate market value of at least US$250 million.

C. Subject to paragraph 2.2 securities issued or guaranteed by a company incorporated in any province of Canada which:

i   are of a class quoted or listed on either the Montreal or the Toronto Stock Exchange;

ii are of a class issued by a company with an equity market capitalisation of at least Can $500 million or a subsidiary of such a company; and

iii are of a class of security having an aggregate market value of at least Can $250 million.

D. Securities or guarantee by a foreign company other than a company referred to in sub-paragraphs a, b and c which:

i   are quoted or listed on an approved foreign stock exchange or which are securities held in Euroclear or CEDEL S.A.;

ii are issued by a company with an equity market capitalisation when translated into sterling of at least £500 million in aggregate or a subsidiary of such a company;

iii are of a class of security having an aggregate market value when translated into sterling of at least £250 million.

E. Securities issued by a government on the approved list which:

i   are quoted or listed on an approved foreign stock exchange; and

ii are of a class of security having an aggregate market value, when translated into sterling of at least £250 million.

F. Subject to paragraph 2.2, US municipal bonds with a Standard and Poor's rating and a Moody's rating of at least AA in each case, and, if only having one such rating, of AA or better.

G. Securities issued by UK investment trusts with a market capitalisation of a least £100 million.

H. Units in UK-authorised unit trusts investing wholly in US Government securities or wholly in cash, or, if more widely invested, with funds under management in excess of £50 million.

I. Units in unit trusts recognised by the Securities and Investment Board as constituting schemes under either section 86 or section 87 of the Financial Services Act 1986, investing wholly in UK or US Government securities or cash, or with funds under management in excess of £50 million or the equivalent in US dollars.

J. Subject to paragraph 2.2, shares in US mutual funds authorised and regulated by the Securities and Exchange Commission with funds under management in excess of US$250 million.

2　**Securities falling within paragraph 1 (b), (c), 2.1 (b), (c), (f) or (j), must be held in Fedwire, the Depository Trust Company (DTC) or the Canadian Depository System (CDS).**

3. Electronically held and traded securities

1　Any US or Canadian government securities, US or Canadian company stocks or UK or foreign securities, which are held and traded electronically in Fedwire, the Depository Trust Company (DTC), the Canadian Depository System (CDS), Euroclear, Cedel S.A. or any depository system mentioned in the definition of approved foreign stock exchange or any other centralised depository available to those trading on the approved foreign stock exchange concerned, may only be comprised in a Lloyd's deposit or Lloyd's life deposit under holding arrangements approved by an authorised person.

2　Any securities to be held in the Central Gilts Office Service or the Central Moneymakers Office Service must be so held under arrangements approved by an authorised person.

4. Guarantees and letters of credit

1　A letter of credit may only be included in a Corporate Member's Lloyd's deposit or Lloyd's life deposit if:

i　it is in the prescribed form;

ii   it has been issued or confirmed by an approved credit institution;

iii it has been issued on the approved credit institution's headed notepaper;

iv   it is encashable in London;

v   it is denominated in either sterling or an approved foreign currency;

vi   unless an authorised person otherwise agrees, it is effective as of 1 January of the year in relation to which it is given;

vii it is clean, irrevocable and valid for an initial period of five years, and subject to automatic extension without written amendment;

viii it is subject to not less than four years' notice of cancellation after the first year;

ix   it is governed by English law and subject to the exclusive jurisdiction of the English courts; and

x   the letter of credit has not been issued on the basis that the collateral (if any) securing the repayment of any amounts paid under the letter of credit comprises directly or indirectly a security interest over a principal private residence.

2   A guarantee may only be included in a Corporate Member's Lloyd's deposit or Lloyd's life deposit if:

i   it is in the prescribed form;

ii   it has been provided by an approved credit institution;

iii it is encashable in London;

iv   it is denominated in either sterling or an approved foreign currency;

v   unless an authorised person otherwise agrees, it is effective as of 1 January of the year in relation to which it is given;

vi   it is valid for an initial period of five years and is subject to not less than four years' notice of cancellation;

vii it is governed by English law and subject to the exclusive jurisdiction of the English courts; and

viii the bank guarantee has not been issued on the basis that the collateral (if any) securing the repayment of any amounts paid under the letter of credit comprises directly or indirectly a security interest over a principal private residence.

3   In the event of the issuing institution having its authority to issue revoked or qualified the Corporate Member will be required to provide a substitute in accordance with the prescribed rules.

4. General restrictions

1   No security may be comprised in a Member's funds at Lloyd's or PTF cash release if it has been issued by:

i   a Corporate Member; or

ii   a company in the same group as a Corporate Member.

2   Bearer securities meeting the criteria set out in paragraph 1 or 2 may be held if either:

i   they are converted into registered form;

ii   the bearer certificates are deposited with an approved financial institution or a nominee company approved by the Council of Lloyd's to act as custodian for the funds at Lloyd's or PTF cash release or a sub-custodian appointed by such custodian; or

iii they are held through a depository or depository system in accordance with the provisions for electronically hand held and traded securities.

3   Partly paid securities may not be comprised in a Member's funds at Lloyd's or PTF cash release.

4   A Corporate Member may not lend securities comprised in its funds at Lloyd's or PTF cash release or documents or evidence of title to such securities.

APPENDIX IV

Glossary

Allocated capacity: that part of a Member's Overall Premium Limit (OPL) which is allocated to syndicates in the relevant year of account.

Active underwriter: the person employed by a managing agent with principal authority to accept risks on behalf of the Members of a syndicate.

Agent: in the context of membership, *see* combined agent, managing agent and members' agent. This term should not be confused with Lloyd's Agents; these are concerned with worldwide shipping intelligence.

Annual solvency test: an examination required under statute of solvency of each Member, matching assets against liabilities at each year end.

Binding authority: an arrangement between an active underwriter of a syndicate and another person (the coverholder), often a broker, under which the coverholder may accept risks within specified parameters on behalf of underwriting Members of the syndicate.

Capacity: the maximum amount of business which may be accepted by a Member (equivalent to his overall premium income limit) or by a syndicate (equivalent to the aggregate of each Member's premium limit on that syndicate).

Capital Structure: the basis on which the regulatory capital, used to support the underwriting of business by syndicates, is provided.

Cash call: a request by the managing agent to the syndicate Members to pay monies to a syndicate to meet claims and expenses. A cash call may be made prior to the normal date of closure of the year of account.

Central Fund: *inter alia* a fund of last resort for the protection of policyholders in the event of a Member being unable to meet his liabilities. The Fund also stands behind CentreWrite Limited and Lioncover Insurance Company Limited. Every Member is required to contribute to the Fund.

CentreWrite Limited: a wholly-owned insurance company established by the Council of Lloyd's in 1991 to reinsure run-off years of account and underwrite estate protection reinsurances.

Closed year: a year of account for which the financial outcome has been determined following its reinsurance with other Lloyd's underwriters of all underwriting liabilities, usually following the third year of an account.

Combined agent: an agent which combines the responsibilities and activities of a Members' agent and a managing agent.

Co-ordinating agent: the Members' agent appointed by Members to co-ordinate their affairs at Lloyd's when underwriting through more than one Members' agent.

Corporate Member: a company incorporated with limited or unlimited liability admitted to membership of the society.

Corporate Syndicate: A syndicate with a single Corporate Member.

Council: the Council of Lloyd's, and any person or delegate acting under its authority, including the Market Board and the Regulatory Board.

Coverholder: A broker or other intermediary who has been granted authority to write risks within certain parameters on behalf of a syndicate.

Dedicated vehicle: a Corporate Member which exclusively supports one or more of the syndicates managed by a particular managing agency. It may be the single Corporate Member of a corporate syndicate or write alongside the Members of a traditional syndicate.

DTI: the UK's Department of Trade and Industry and/or insofar as the context implies, the Secretary of State for Trade and Industry.

Drop: the amount of capacity that reverts to the managing agent of a syndicate from members who resign, reduce their commitment or decline to take a pre-emption offer and do not sell their capacity through the auction..

Earmarking: Taking credit from the Central Fund on behalf of a Member when there are insufficient funds in that Member's Premium Trust Funds or funds at Lloyd's to cover the Member's liabilities.

Equitas Reinsurance Limited: A DTI authorised Reinsurance company which has underwritten the reinsurance of all the liabilities, in relation to 1992 and prior underwriting years of account, of all members of all Lloyd's syndicates (except Life Syndicates).

Funds at Lloyd's: funds lodged and held in trust at Lloyd's as security for the policyholders and to support a Member's overall underwriting activities. The amount is related to a Member's premium income limit, in accordance with the ratios laid down by the Council of Lloyd's. The administration of these funds is subject to the various Trust

Deeds and regulatory requirements. The funds must be in a form approved by the Council of Lloyd's and be maintained in value.

IBNR (Incurred But Not Reported): claims arising from accidents or events which have occurred or are statistically predicted to occur but which have yet to be advised.

ICA: Insurance Companies Act 1982 (UK).

Inception date accounting: for accounting purposes a system whereby risks underwritten are allocated to the year of account in which the period of cover commences.

Insurance carrier: a company which itself or through a subsidiary carries on insurance or reinsurance business other than Lloyd's.

Integrated Lloyd's Vehicle (ILV): a company which owns or controls a dedicated vehicle supporting one or more continuous syndicates and the managing agency.

Interavailability: involves making funds at Lloyd's available to support both the past underwriting of a Member and the future underwriting of that same Member's successor Corporate Member.

Line: the proportion of a risk accepted by an underwriter. Also used to refer to the amount which an underwriter has fixed as his maximum exposure for any one risk.

Lioncover Insurance Company Limited: a wholly-owned insurance company formed by the Council of Lloyd's in 1987 to reinsure the liabilities of certain Lloyd's syndicates.

Lloyd's adviser: an adviser (registered under the Lloyd's Advisers Bye-law) retained by a Corporate Member for syndicate analysis and negotiation of syndicate participations pursuant to the Membership Bye-law.

Lloyd's broker: a partnership or corporate body permitted by the Council of Lloyd's to broke insurance business at Lloyd's.

Lloyd's Central Accounting: a central accounting facility provided by the Corporation of Lloyd's enabling syndicates and brokers to receive or pay money centrally.

Lloyd's deposit: a deposit held subject to the terms of the Lloyd's Deposit Trust Deed and forming part of a Member's funds at Lloyd's.

Lloyd's Policy Signing Office (LPSO): a central service provided by the Corporation of Lloyd's. Its main functions are to check, validate and record transactions, check and sign policies on behalf of Members and operate Lloyd's central accounting.

Long-tail: a term used to describe insurance business where it is known from experience that notification and settlement of claims may take many years.

LPSO: Lloyd's Policy Signing Office (*see this glossary*).

Managing agent: an agent responsible for managing a syndicate and employing the active underwriter.

Managing agents' agreement: a contract, in a form prescribed by Lloyd's, between a Member and its managing agent, which sets out the duties, powers and remuneration of the managing agent and the obligations of the Member.

MAPA: Members' Agents' Pooling Arrangements (see below).

Members' Agents' Pooling Arrangements (MAPA): an arrangement allowing Members to participate in a wider range of syndicates than normally possible, thereby spreading the risk over larger numbers of syndicates.

Means: the level of wealth a Member must prove to commence or continue underwriting. The means shown must be maintained in value at all times, must be in an approved form and may be subject to reconfirmation.

Member: in the context of this guide, an individual underwriting at Lloyd's with unlimited liability, unless otherwise specified as referring to a Corporate Member underwriting with limited liability.

Members' agent: an agent to whom a (usually individual) Member delegates control of his Lloyd's affairs other than the underwriting.

Members' Agent Agreement: a contract in a form prescribed by Lloyd's, between a (usually individual) Member and the Member's agent which sets out the duties, powers and remuneration of the Members' agent and obligations of the Member.

Members' Agent's Information Report (MAIR): a document produced yearly containing such information as would materially assist a prospective Member to make an informed assessment of the Members' agent and its business.

Name: the traditional term for a Member of Lloyd's.

Open year: a year of account which has not been closed, which usually occurs at the end of the third year, and to which adjustments continue to be made. A year of account can be left open beyond the third year if the extent of the liability cannot be accurately quantified.

OPL: Overall Premium Limit (*see this glossary*).

Outstanding losses or claims: the total losses or claims which have been advised, but are yet to be paid and are only estimated amounts.

Overall Premium Limit (or Overall Premium Income Limit) (OPL): the maximum amount of business which a Member may underwrite based on the level of his or her funds at Lloyd's.

Pre-emption Rights: the right of any member of a syndicate to participate in any increase of that syndicate's capacity on a pro-rata basis.

Premiums Trust Fund (PTF): trust funds into which all premiums received by a Member or by managing agents on behalf of a Member must be placed and which are available for the payment of reinsurance premiums, claims and syndicate and other expenses and, when the year of account has been closed, profits to Members. Each Member has three funds: a sterling fund, a US dollar fund (known as a Lloyd's American Trust Fund) and a Canadian dollar fund (known as a Lloyd's Canadian Trust Fund).

'Quota Share Arrangement': a reinsurance agreement whereby the reinsurer cedes a predetermined proportion of all business (or specified part thereof) to his reinsurers.

Regulatory capital: the capital which is deposited as funds at Lloyd's and which is used to satisfy the requirements under insurance legislation for underwriters to maintain a required solvency margin.

Reinsurance-to-close (RITC): a reinsurance agreement under which underwriting Members who are Members of a syndicate for a year of account to be closed are reinsured by (usually) underwriting Members who comprise that of another syndicate for a later year of account against all liabilities arising out of insurance business underwritten by the reinsured syndicate.

Riesco: a basis for allocating calendar year investment income and appreciation to two or more years of account by reference to the average value of the funds for each of those years of account.

Run-off account: a year of account of a syndicate which has ceased to trade.

Short-tail: business on which claims generally arise and are settled quickly.

Society: the Society and Corporation of Lloyd's.

Split syndicate: the traditional syndicate and corporate syndicate with it writes in parallel, taken together.

Successor Corporate Member: a Corporate Member, the whole of the equity share capital of which is beneficially owned by individual Members who have entered into an approved conversion arrangement with that Corporate Member.

Syndicate: a group of Members on behalf of whom an active underwriter accepts insurance business.

Summary Annual Report: a report containing summarised highlights of the syndicate annual report (SAR) which may be produced (in addition/as an alternative to) the SAR.

Syndicate Annual Report (SAR): an obligatory annual financial report to Members, in a prescribed format, showing the state of affairs of each supported syndicate. Attached to the report are the reports of the managing agent, active underwriter and syndicate auditor, together with disclosure information.

Syndicate stamp: a document which must be registered with Lloyd's setting out the names and participations of the Members of a syndicate.

Traditional syndicate: a syndicate comprised of several members, whether individual or corporate, formed from year to year.

Transition: an arrangement whereby the Member transfers the whole of his continuing underwriting business at Lloyd's (by the reinsurance of all open and run-off years) to a Corporate Member.

Underwriting agent: see combined agent, managing agent and Members' agent.

Year of account: the basic accounting period at Lloyd's (*see* Inception date accounting).

APPENDIX V
Corporate Figures

New Corporate Members for 1994

Company	No of Mems	Type	Capital Raised £m	Allocated Capacity 1994 £m	UK Institutions £m	Lloyd's Related £m	Non-US Insurance Industry £m	US Insurance Industry £m	US Insurance Venture Capital £m	US Institution £m	Overseas Investors £m	Sponsor/Broker Backer	Members' Agent Lloyd's Adviser
London Insurance Market Investment Trust plc	10	Listed spread vehicle	280.00	502.50	280.00							Samuel Montagu/ James Capel	LIMIT Advisers
CLM Insurance Fund plc	10	Listed spread vehicle	86.00	154.00	86.00							BZW	CLM Advisers
Angerstein Underwriting Trust plc	10	Listed spread vehicle	67.00	112.80	67.00							NatWest Markets	Stace Barr
HCG Lloyd's Investment Trust plc	6	Listed spread vehicle	65.00	96.00	65.00							JO Hambro/UBS	HCG Advisers
New London Capital plc	5	Listed spread vehicle	60.00	105.00	60.00							SG Warburg/ Warburg Securities	Chartwell Advisers
Delian Lloyd's Investment Trust plc	7	Listed spread vehicle	51.00	95.00	51.00							Hill Samuel/ Panmure Gordon	RF Kershaw
Masthead Insurance Underwriting plc	5	Listed spread vehicle	40.00	71.60	40.00							Hambros/Hoare Govett	Murray Lawrence
Premium Underwriting plc	5	Listed spread vehicle	33.00	62.00	33.00							Noble & Co/Greig Middleton	Wellington
Syndicate Capital Trust plc	5	Listed spread vehicle	32.00	60.00	32.00							Raphael Zorm Hemsley	Insurance Analysis
Abtrust Lloyd's Insurance Trust plc	5	Listed spread vehicle	30.00	38.30	30.00							Peel Hunt	Bankside
Finsbury Underwriting Investment Trsut plc	5	Listed spread vehicle	30.00	50.00	30.00							Rea Bros/UBS	Wren
Hiscox Select Insurance Fund plc	5	Listed spread vehicle	30.00	49.60	30.00							Charterhouse Tilney	Hiscox
Lomond Underwriting plc	5	Spread vehicle	27.00	54.00	27.00							Murray Johnstone	Willis Faber
Navigators Corporate Underwriters Ltd	1	Spread vehicle	19.29	38.50				9.65		9.64		Brown Brothers Harriman	Murray Lawrence
Camperdown Corporation	1	Spread vehicle	14.13	28.25				14.13				St Paul's	Camperdown
Hiscox Dedicated Corporate Member Ltd	1	Dedicated	10.25	20.50	7.85	2.40						Charterhouse Tilney	Hiscox Syndicates
ABSA Syndicate Investments Ltd	1	Spread vehicle	6.50	13.00							6.50	ABSA	Wellington
Duncanson & Holt Underwriters Ltd	1	Spread vehicle	5.10	8.50				5.10				Unum Group	Duncanson & Holt
Athanor Ltd	1	Spread vehicle	5.00	10.00							5.00	Brederode	Stace Barr
Wentworth Underwriting Ltd	1	Spread vehicle	5.00	10.00							5.00	Tsavliris Group	Sedgwick
Kiln Cotesworth Corporate Member Ltd	1	Spread vehicle	2.25	4.50	2.25							Baring Bros	Kiln
Yasuda Lloyd's Corporate Member Ltd	1	Spread vehicle	1.50	2.10			1.50					Yasuda	Kiln
Mical Ltd	1	Spread vehicle	1.50	3.00		1.50						Miller	Murray Lawrence
Gregory & Partners Ltd	1	Spread vehicle	1.50	3.00		1.50							Jardine
Trust Underwriting Ltd	1	Spread vehicle	1.50	3.00		1.50							Christie Brockbank
Totals	**95**		**904.52**	**1,595.15**	**841.10**	**6.90**	**1.50**	**28.88**	**0.00**	**9.64**	**16.50**		

Information Source: Lloyd's

New Corporate Members for 1995

Company	No of Membs	Type	Capital raised £m	Allocated Capacity £m	UK Institutions £m	Lloyd's Related £m	Non-US Insurance Industry £m	US Insurance Industry £m	US Insurance Industry £m	US Institutions £m	Overseas Investors £m	Sponsor/Broker/Backer	Managing Agent/Members' Agent
Wellington Underwriting plc	5	Listed dedicated	17.25	32.00	3.65	9.33				1.27	3.00	Noble & Co/ Greig Middleton	Wellington
Hiscox Dedicated Insurance Fund plc	1	Dedicated	26.62	37.00	11.85				14.77			Charterhouse Tilney/ Trident	Hiscox
Venton Underwriting Ltd	1	Dedicated	13.50	24.54					13.50			Trident	Venton
Venton Underwriting Group Ltd	1	Dedicated	5.00	9.09							5.00	Bank of Butterfield	Venton
Hardy Underwriting plc	1	Dedicated	2.85	5.00	1.85	1.00						Noble & Co	Hardy
Liberty Corporate Capital Ltd	1	Corp syndicate	40.00	40.00				40.00				Liberty Mutual	Cater Allen (Syndicate 190)
Matheson Lloyd's Investment Trust plc	7	Listed spread vehicle	25.00	38.00	6.75						18.25	Swiss Bank	Jardine
Euclidian plc	6	Listed spread vehicle	20.00	80.00	18.40			1.60				Samuel Montagu/ Charterhouse Tilney	Indemnity Insurance Services
MIEC Investment Company Inc	1	Spread vehicle	2.24	4.48				2.24				Medical Underwriters of California	Stace Barr
Kiln Capital plc	1	Listed dedicated	25.49	47.86	22.16	0.43			2.90			Morgan Stanley/Cazenove	Kiln
Frankona Capital Ltd	1	Corp syndicate	6.50	10.00			6.50					Frankona	Cater Allen (Syndicate 322)
Nissan Lloyd's Underwriting Ltd	1	Spread vehicle	2.50	5.00			2.50					Nissan Fire & Marine Insurance Co Ltd	Wellington
Archer Dedicated plc	1	Dedicated	4.00	7.50	4.00							UBS	Archer
Tarquin Underwriters Ltd	1	Corp syndicate	88.00	160.00					88.00			Salomon Brothers Insurance Ptnrs/Harvard	Charman
Atrium Capital Limited	1	Dedicated	3.00	5.26	1.00	2.00							Atrium
D P M Corporate Name Ltd	1	Dedicated	1.50	2.31		1.50							D P Mann
Cox Dedicated Corporate Member Ltd	1	Listed dedicated	12.00	22.25	6.00			6.00				Raphael Zorn Hemsley	Cox
RGB Capital Holdings Ltd	2	Corp syndicate	9.50	17.53			9.50					Noble & Co/Frankona	RGB
Advent Capital plc	1	Dedicated	1.65	1.10		1.65							B F Caudle
SCC at Lloyd's Ltd	1	Spread vehicle	1.50	3.00							1.50		Christopherson Heath
Equity Red Star Ltd	1	Corp syndicate	1.75	3.18		1.75							Christopherson Heath
ZIC Lloyd's Underwriting Ltd	1	Dedicated	3.20	4.57				3.20				Zenith Insurance Company	Sturge (Syndicate 219)
Sextant Corporate Member Ltd	1	Dedicated	1.50	3.00		1.50							Murray Lawrence
North American London Underwriters	1	Spread vehicle	9.10	14.00				9.10					Wren Lloyd's Advisers
Mears Incorporated Capital Ltd	1	Spread vehicle	1.70	3.39		1.70						R Mears & Co Ltd	Syndicate Advisers
Windford Company Ltd	1	Spread vehicle	1.50	3.00		1.50							Barder & Marsh
LB Ltd	1	Spread vehicle	1.50	3.00		1.50							Falcoln
Damillo Ltd	1	Spread vehicle	1.50	3.00		1.50						2 Transitional Names	Anton
Sumac Underwriting (UK) Ltd	1	Spread vehicle	1.50	3.00		1.50							Murray Lawrence
Totals	**45**		**331.35**	**592.06**	**75.66**	**26.86**	**18.50**	**62.14**	**119.17**	**1.27**	**27.75**		

Information Source: Lloyd's

New Corporate Members for 1996

Company	No of Membs	Type	Capital raised £m	Allocated Capacity £m	UK Institutions £m	Lloyd's Related £m	Non-US Insurance Industry £m	US Insurance Industry £m	US Insurance Industry £m	US Institutions £m	Overseas Investors £m	Financial adviser/Backer	Managing Agent or Lloyd's Adviser/Managing Agent
County Down Ltd/Dornoch Ltd	2	Parallel syndicates (2)	50.00	100.00			50.00					Mid Ocean	Brockbank
Terra Nova Capital Ltd	1	Dedicated vehicle	12.50	25.00			12.50					Terra Nova	Octavian
CNA Corporate Capital Ltd	1	Parallel syndicates (4)	12.50	25.00				12.50				CNA International	
SVB Underwriting Ltd	1	Dedicated vehicle	3.15	5.25		3.15							Spreckley Villers Burnhope
Ockham London Ltd/Ockham Direct Ltd	2	Dedicated vehicle	1.00	2.00		1.00							Sturge
Catlin Westgen Ltd	1	Parallel syndicate (1)	25.50	51.00			25.50					Western General Insurance, Lehman Brothers	Catlin
Camperdown UK Ltd	1	Parallel synds (2) / spread vehicle	14.50	23.00				14.50				The St Paul Companies	
NLC Name No 7 Ltd	1	Additional corporate member for existing spread vehicle	7.50	15.00				7.50					Chartwell Advisers
QBE Corporate Ltd	1	Parallel syndicate (1)	20.50	22.63			20.50					QBE	QBE Underwriting Agency Ltd
Lumley Underwriting Ltd	1	Dedicated vehicle	1.50	3.00			1.50					Edward Lumley Holdings	Bates Cunningham
Stewart Dedicated Ltd	1	Dedicated vehicle	5.00	10.00		5.00							Stewart Syndicates
Premium Eta Ltd/Premium Zeta Ltd	2	Additional corporate members for existing spread vehicle	15.00	13.91	15.00							Noble & Co	Wellington Member Agency
Millenium Underwriting Ltd	1	Dedicated vehicle	0.90	1.50		0.90							Mander, Thomas & Cooper
Jago Capital Ltd	1	Dedicated vehicle	1.50	2.73		1.50							Jago Managing Agency
F&G UK Underwriters Ltd	1	Stand alone corporate syndicate	11.60	17.84				11.60				USF&G	F&G UK Agency Ltd
Citadel Underwriting Ltd	1	Spread vehicle	2.00	4.00			2.00					Citadel Insurance, Littlejohn Frazer	Barder & Marsh
Goshawk Syndicate Ltd	1	Dedicated vehicle	0.55	0.85		0.55							Gammell Kershaw
Calenden Ltd	1	Spread vehicle	0.50	0.75		0.50							Sedgwick Lloyd's Underwriting Agents
ACE Capital Ltd	1	Dedicated vehicle	12.25	24.50			12.25						Methuen
Plus 1 other unannounced	1		0.92	1.84		0.92							
Totals	**23**		**198.87**	**349.80**	**15.00**	**13.52**	**124.25**	**46.10**	**0.00**	**0.00**	**0.00**		

Information Source: Lloyd's

New Corporate Members for the 1997 year of account

Company	Members Agent	Type	Allocated Capacity 1997 £m	Backer
ACE Staff Corporate Member Ltd	N	Dedicated	0.86	ACE Limited 100%
Chariot Underwriting Plc	Y	Listed conversion vehicle	1.87	- - - - -
Cotesworth Dedicated Ltd	N	Dedicated	14.5	Walsham Brothers and Co 45%
CRC Capital Ltd	N	Dedicated	39.75	Capital Re Corporation 100%
Crowe Corporate Capital Ltd	N	Dedicated	38	New London Capital plc 52%
Devon Underwriting Ltd	Y	Conversion	0.6	
East Yorkshire Underwriters (Wren) Ltd	Y	Conversion	3.91	
Forum Underwriting Ltd	Y	Spread vehicle	2.1	Crowe Investors Ltd 100%
Global Capital Underwriting Ltd	N	Dedicated	6.5	Global Capital Reinsurance Holdings Ltd 100%
Grenville Underwriting Plc	Y	Conversion	9.47	- - - - -
Hardy Names Ltd	N	Conversion	7.71	Hardy Underwriting Group 100%
Heraldglen Ltd	N	Dedicated	33.93	TIG Holdings 80% / AON
Holywell (Wren) Ltd	Y	Conversion	0.91	
KS (Wren) Ltd	Y	Conversion	1.03	
LaSalle Re Corporate Capital Ltd	N	Spread vehicle	16.33	LaSalle Re Holdings Ltd 100%
MFB Corporate Member Ltd	Y	Conversion	2.98	MFB Capital plc 100%
Navigators Corporate Underwriters Ltd	N	Targetted spread vehicle	34	
North West Names Ltd	Y	Conversion	.71	
Oak Dedicated Ltd	N	Dedicated	33.81	Charwell Re Corporation 100%
P R Maguire Ltd	Y	Conversion	0.2	
PX Re Ltd	N	Corporate syndicate	35	PXRE Corporation 100%
RGA Capital Ltd	N	Dedicated	2.79	General American Life Insurance Co 100%
Service Corporate Capital Ltd	N	Dedicated	17.96	Phoenix Securities 100%
Syndicate 457 Capital Ltd	N	Dedicated	39.06	
TIG Corporate Name (No 1) Ltd	N	Corporate syndicate	20	TIG Holdings Inc 100%
Torch Dedicated Corporate Member Ltd	N	Dedicated	9.3	SCT / BRIT 50% / 50%
Two Churches (Underwriting) Ltd	Y	Conversion	1.03	
Yeh-Lloyd's Partners Ltd	Y	Conversion	3	

1997 Corporate Members (all)

Company	First year of Underwriting	Spread Capacity £m	Dedicated Capacity £m	Corporate Syndicate Capacity £m	Conversion Spread Capacity £m	Conversion Dedicated Capacity £m	1997 Total Capacity £m
Atrium Capital Ltd (609 Capital Ltd)	95	0	7.20	0	0	0	7.20
ABSA Syndicate Investments Ltd	94	18.75	0	0	0	0	18.75
ACE Limited	96	0	142.43	0	0	0	142.43
ACE Staff Corporate Member Ltd	97	0	0.86	0	0	0	0.86
ADIT One Ltd	95	0	41.50	0	0	0	41.50
Advent Capital plc	95	0	7.50	0	0	0	7.50
Abtrust Lloyd's Investment Trust plc	94	0	53.22	0	0	0	53.22
Athanor Ltd	94	0	13.01	0	0	0	13.01
Angerstein Underwriting Trust plc	94	0	197.16	0	0	0	197.16
Brora SLP	97	0	0	0	5.03	0	5.03
Calenden Ltd	96	0	0.72	0	0	0	0.72
The St Paul Companies Inc (Camperdown)	96	0	58	57.50	0	0	57.50
Catlin Westgen Ltd	96	0	122	121.99	0	0	121.99
Chariot Underwriting Plc	97	0	0	0	1.87	0	1.87
Chaucer Dedicated Ltd (formerly Stewart)	96	0	10.00	0	0	0	10.00
Citadel Underwriting Ltd	96	4.86	0	0	0	0	4.86
CLM Insurance Fund plc	94	205.00	0	0	0	0	205.00
CNA Corp Capital Ltd	96	0	47.97	0	0	0	47.97
Cotesworth Dedicated Ltd	97	0	4.50	0	0	0	14.50
Mid Ocean (County Down/Dornoch)	96	0	142.06	0	0	0	142.06
Cox plc	95	0	133.65	0	0	0	133.65
CRC Capital Limited	97	0	39.75	0	0	0	39.75
Crowe Corporate Capital Limited	97	0	38.00	0	0	0	38.00
Damillo Ltd	95	2.66	0	0	0	0	2.66
Devon Underwriting Limited	97	0	0	0	0.60	0	0.60
DPM Corporate Name Ltd	95	0	27.50	0	0	0	27.50
Duncanson & Holt Underwriters Ltd	96	98.85	0	0	0	0	98.85
East Yorkshire Underwriters (Wren) Ltd	97	0	0	0	3.91	0	3.91
Euclidian plc	95	98.90	0	0	0	0	98.90
F&G UK Ltd	96	0	5.00	17.84	0	0	22.84
Forum Underwriting Limited	97	2.10	0	0	0	0	2.10
Frankona Capital Ltd	95	0	12.03	0	0	0	12.03
Finsbury Underwriting Investment Trust plc	94	70.07	0	0	0	0	70.07
Global Capital Underwriting Limited	97	0	6.50	0	0	0	6.50
Goshawk Dedicated Ltd	96	0	14.61	0	0	0	14.61
Gregory & Partners Ltd	96	5.00	0	0	0	0	5.00
Grenville Underwriting Plc	97	0	0	0	9.47	0	9.47
Hardy Names Limited	97	0	0	0	0	7.71	7.71
Hardy Underwriting plc	95	0	8.32	0	0	0	8.32
HCG Lloyd's Investment Trust plc	94	127.59	0	0	0	0	127.59
Helmsdale SLP	97	0	0	0	7.04	0	7.04
Heraldglen Limited	97	0	33.93	0	0	0	33.93
Hiscox Dedicated Corp Member Ltd	94	0	58.66	0	0	0	58.66
Hiscox Select Insurance Fund plc	94	57.79	0	0	0	0	57.79
Holywell (Wren) Limited	97	0	0	0	0.91	0	0.91
Jago Capital Ltd	96	0	4.83	0	0	0	4.83
Kiln Cotesworth Corp Member Ltd	94	5.00	0	0	0	0	5.00
Kiln Cotesworth SLP 1	97	0	0	0	4.34	0	4.34
Kiln Underwriting Ltd	95	0	54.80	0	0	0	58.80
KS (Wren) Limited	97	0	0	0	1.03	0	1.03

LaSalle Re Corporate Capital Limited	97	16.33	0	0	0	0	16.33
LB Ltd	95	5.34	0	0	0	0	5.34
Liberty Corporate Capital Ltd	95	0	0	185.00	0	0	185.00
London Insurance Market Investment Trust plc	94	648.00	0	0	0	0	648.00
Lomond Underwriting plc	94	102.00	0	0	0	0	102.00
Lumley Underwriting Ltd	96	0	5.30	0	0	0	5.30
Masthead Insurance Underwriting plc	94	74.58	0	0	0	0	74.58
MFB Corporate Member Limited	97	0	0	0	2.98	0	2.98
MIEC Investment Company Inc	95	4.65	0	0	0	0	4.65
Millenium Underwriting Ltd	96	0	12.65	0	0	0	12.65
Matheson Lloyd's Investment Trust plc	95	38.50	0	0	0	0	38.50
N American London Underwriters Ltd	95	49.20	0	0	0	0	49.20
Navigators Corporate Underwriters Ltd	97	34.00	0	0	0	0	34.00
Nissan Lloyd's Underwriting Ltd	95	3.39	0	2.10	0	0	5.49
New London Capital plc	94	134.29	0	2.10	0	0	134.29
North West Names Limited	97	0	0	0	0.71	0	0.71
Oak Dedicated Limited	97	0	32.81	0	0	0	32.81
Ockham Direct Ltd	96	0	44.16	0	0	0	44.16
PR Maguire Limited	97	0	0	0	0.20	0	0.20
Premium Underwriting plc	94	0	76.58	0	0	0	76.58
Private SLPs (Roberts & Hiscox)	97	0	0	0	1.54	0	1.54
Private SLPs (Murray Lawrence)	97	0	0	0	11.90	0	11.90
Private SLPs (Kiln Cotesworth)	97	0	0	0	8.13	0	8.13
PX Re Limited	97	0	0	35.00	0	0	35.00
QBE Corporate Ltd	96	0	34	25.00	0	0	59.08
RGA Capital Limited	97	0	2.79	0	0	0	2.79
RGB Capital	0	0	22.73	0	0	0	22.73
Riverside Corporate Underwriters Ltd	94	26.76	0	0	0	0	26.76
SCC at Lloyd's Ltd	96	7.68	0	0	0	0	7.68
Service Corporate Capital Limited	97	0	17.96	0	0	0	17.96
Sextant Corporate Member Ltd	95	0	51.60	0	0	0	51.60
Stewart Plus SLP 1	97	0	0	0	2.62	0	2.62
Sumac Underwriting (UK) Ltd	95	2.34	0	0	0	0	2.34
SVB Underwriting Ltd	96	0	12.01	0	0	0	12.01
Syndicate 457 Capital Limited	97	0	39.06	0	0	0	39.06
Syndicate Capital Trust plc	94	65.14	0	0	0	0	65.14
Tarquin Underwriters Ltd	95	0	200.16	0	0	0	200.16
Terra Nova Capital Ltd	96	0	102.70	81.00	0	0	183.70
The Murray Lawrence Group 1 SLP	97	0	0	0	223	0	2.23
The Murray Lawrence Group 2 SLP	97	0	0	0	1.90	0	1.90
TIG Corporate Name (No 1) Limited	97	0	0	20.00	0	0	20.00
Torch dedicated Corporate Member Ltd	97	0	9.30	0	0	0	9.30
Trust Underwriting Ltd	94	3.56	0	0	0	0	3.56
Two Churches (Underwriting) Limited	97	0	0	0	1.03	0	1.03
Yeh-Lloyd's Partners Limited	97	0	0	0	3.00	0	3.00
Venton Underwriting Group Ltd	95	0	10.06	0	0	0	10.06
Venton Underwriting Ltd	95	0	51.75	40.00	0	0	91.75
Wellington Underwriting plc	95	0	65.75	0	0	0	65.75
Windford Company Ltd	95	3.85	0	0	0	0	3.85
Yasuda Lloyd's Corp Member Ltd	94	2.02	0	0	0	0	2.02
ZIC Lloyd's Underwriting Ltd	95	0	5.05	0	0	0	5.05
One unannounced	96	6.46	0	0	0	0	6.46
TOTALS		**2,265.36**	**1,750.99**	**405.94**	**70.44**	**7.71**	**4,500.45**

NB *Many listed spread vehicles now have stakes in managing agents, and a proportion of their capacity could therefore be said to be "dedicated". This has not, however, been reflected above.*

Analysis of Managing Agent Alignment

Managing Agent (Includes transactions where formal completion has not yet taken place)

Managing Agent	Managed Capacity (£000)	Agency Backer(s)	Type - principal backer	Alignment type (if no agency control)	% equity in managing agency	% managed capacity provided by aligned corporate	
Active Syndicate Management Limited	27,419	Berkshire Hathaway	US Insurance		33%	108.32%	*
ACE London Aviation Limited	204,080	ACE	Bermudan Insurance		100%	0.62%	
ACE London Underwriting Ltd	157,331	ACE	Bermudan Insurance		100%	9.05%	
Methuen (Lloyd's Underwriting Agents) Ltd	383,485	ACE	Bermudan Insurance		100%	33.10%	
AE Grant (Underwriting Agencies) Ltd	58,894	Riverside group	US Insurance		0%	13.16%	
Apollo Underwriting Ltd	71,386	Various reinsurers	US Insurance/Non-US/Bermudan Insurance	x	0%	54.71%	+
Archer Managing Agents Limited	380,437	Chartwell Re	US Insurance		100%	19.53%	#
Ashley Palmer Limited	181,734	F&G	US Insurance		80%	12.57%	++#
Bankside Syndicates Ltd	422,012	LIMIT	UK Institutions		65%	22.51%	
Brockbank Personal Lines Ltd	889,38	Mid Ocean	Bermudan Insurance		51%	55.55%	
Brockbank Syndicate Management Ltd	426,358	Mid Ocean	Bermudan Insurance		51%	21.73%	
Cassidy Davis Syndicate Management Ltd	727,58	St Paul	US Insurance		100%	27.62%	
Catlin Underwriting Agencies Ltd	196,666	Catlin Westgen Ltd	Bermudan Insurance		75%	62.03%	
Charman Underwriting Agencies Ltd	330,181	Tarquin	US Insurance venture capital		100%	60.62%	
Kingsmead Underwriting Agency Limited (formerly Claremount)	179,479	TIG/AON	US Insurance		100%	18.91%	
CNA Underwriting Agencies Ltd	25,000	CNA	US Insurance		100%	100.00%	
Cox Group managing agencies	271,215	Cox Plc	UK Institutions/US Insurance venture capital		100%	44.12%	
Christopherson Heath	212,491	Cox plc	UK Institutions/US Insurance venture capital		100%	6.59%	
Crowe Syndicate Management Ltd	220,410	NLC	UK Institutions	xx	20%	19.85%	
DP Mann Underwriting Agency Limited	234,210	Chase Manhattan/Others	US Insurance venture capital	xxx	40%	11.74%	
Duncanson & Holt Syndicate Management Ltd	108,225	D&H Europe	US Insurance		100%	44.16%	
Trafalgar Underwriting Agencies	54,424	D&H Europe	US Insurance		100%	18.83%	
Gammell Kershaw	86,107	Goshawk Insurance Holdings Plc (c.40% Synd. Capital Trust)	UK Institutions		100%	16.96%	
Gravett & Tilling (Syndicate Management) Ltd	157,941	St Paul	US Insurance		100%	11.66%	
Hiscox Syndicates Ltd	370,469	Hiscox plc (33% Trident)	UK Institutions (Bermudan insurance)		100%	15.83%	
J E Mumford (Underwriting Agencies) Ltd	76,248	Angerstein	UK Institutions		100%	6.16%	
Jago Managing Agency Ltd	121,020	Unionamerica/AON	US Insurance		57%	3.99%	
Janson Green Ltd	325,548	LIMIT	UK Institutions		70%	10.14%	
CLM Managing Agency Ltd	44,887	CLM	UK Institutions		100%	90.74%	
Liberty Syndicate Management Ltd	185,000	Liberty	US Insurance		100%	100.00%	
Ockham Personal Insurance Agency Ltd	217,975	Questor	US Insurance venture capital		33%	20.26%	
Octavian Syndicate Management Ltd	388,101	Terra Nova	Bermudan Insurance		100%	47.33%	
Owen & Wilby Underwriting Agency Ltd	51,117	NALU/D&H Europe	US Insurance	x	0%	87.00%	
PB Coffey (Underwriting Agency)	37,658	Angerstein	UK Institutions		100%	14.07%	
PXRE Managing Agency Ltd	35,000	PX Re	US Insurance		100%	100.00%	
QBE Underwriting Agency Ltd	63,500	QBE	Non-US Insurance		100%	93.04%	
RGB Underwriting Agencies Ltd	128,833	Capital Re Corporation	US Insurance		100%	30.85%	
Service Managing Agency Ltd	32,959	Phoenix	UK Institutions		100%	54.48%	
Spreckley Villers Burnhope & Co Ltd	224,455	AON/Strategic Partners	US Insurance		40%	5.35%	
Chaucer Syndicates Ltd (formerly Stewart Syndicates Ltd)	217,537	BRIT/Electra	UK Institutions		50%	7.01%	
TIG Syndicate Management	20,000	TIG Re	US Insurance		100%	100.00%	
Venton Underwriting Agencies Ltd	225,550	Trident	Bermudan Insurance		63%	40.68%	
Wellington Underwriting Agencies Ltd	603,083	Wellington	UK Institutions		100%	10.90%	
Wren Syndicate Management Ltd	293,967	BRIT/FUIT	UK Institutions	xxx	25%	14.97%	
Total 1997 Aligned Capacity	8,214,089					27.10%	
Total 1997 Market Capacity	10,323,602						

* - via DTI approved company with parallel consortium arrangement in place - all risks 94% ASM, 6% co-insurers (synd 962), 38.75% ASM, 61.25% co-insurers (synd 892)
+ - Negotiations continuing re: proposed stake
++ - Includes capacity provided by ADIT and Oak Dedicated

Information Source: Lloyd's